Sharing a laugh?

A qualitative study of mentoring interventions with young people

Kate Philip, Janet Shucksmith and Caroline King

JR
JOSEPH
ROWNTREE
FOUNDATION
1904
2004

The **Joseph Rowntree Foundation** has supported this project as part of its programme of research and innovative development projects, which it hopes will be of value to policy makers, practitioners and service users. The facts presented and views expressed in this report are, however, those of the authors and not necessarily those of the Foundation.

Joseph Rowntree Foundation
The Homestead
40 Water End
York YO30 6WP
Website: www. jrf.org.uk

UNIVERSITY
OF ABERDEEN

The Rowan Group is a new focus for policy related research on young people's education and general well-being. It builds on a long tradition of work in this vein carried out under the banner of the Centre for Educational Research.

Cover design by Adkins Design

Prepared and printed by:
York Publishing Services Ltd
64 Hallfield Road
Layerthorpe
York YO31 7ZQ
Tel: 01904 430033; Fax: 01904 430868; Website: www.yps-publishing.co.uk

Further copies of this report, or any other JRF publication, can be obtained either from the JRF website (www.jrf.org.uk/bookshop/) or from our distributor, York Publishing Services Ltd, at the above address.

Contents

Acknowledgements

The authors wish to acknowledge the dedicated support given by the three mentoring projects that participated in the study: Covesea Intensive Housing Project, Pinefield Education Centre and Dundee Youth-Link Befriending Project. Staff, management and volunteers all gave generously of their time and helped with the research in numerous ways for which we are very grateful. In addition staff at Aberlour Childcare Trust also deserve thanks for their help. We would also like to thank the many people within local authority departments, voluntary organisations, community groups and health services who helped with the research.

We are also grateful for the valuable contributions made to this study by the Joseph Rowntree Foundation's Advisory Group, comprising of Helen Colley, Alastair Delaney, Stella Everingham, Andy Furlong, Simon Jaquet, Charlie Lloyd, Mike Nicholson and Mike Stein. Particular thanks go to Charlie Lloyd our research link with JRF who provided encouragement and constructive criticism throughout the project. Helen Colley was a constant support and critical friend to the research team.

We would also like to thank Marjorie Reilly, Sally Scott and Alison Moir in the Department of Sociology for their help with the many tasks they undertook in supporting the project. And of course our colleagues in the Rowan Group for coffee, comments and support. Particular thanks go to Dod Forrest for reading and commenting on early drafts of this report.

Above all, we wish to thank the young people who participated in the study at the different stages. We hope that this report does justice to your accounts.

1 Young people and planned mentoring

Young people growing up in western societies have to deal with a rapidly changing social world that differs markedly from that experienced by previous generations (Coles, 2001). Research has consistently shown that these changes have their strongest impact on those with the least resources and who are most likely to be defined as vulnerable. Current investigations of patterns of social exclusion with young people have highlighted the complex relationships between different kinds of inequalities. Yet we still know little of the realities of how young people in such settings move in and out of 'risk' and why some groups of young people appear to be able to make a success of their lives, despite facing a range of adverse circumstances.

A growing body of work, much of it based on North American studies, has suggested that the presence of an adult mentor can be valuable in helping young people through the processes of transition to adulthood. Commentators have also suggested that the presence of a long-term caring adult may be an important 'steeling mechanism' in helping young people to resist adverse circumstances. Much of this work has been based on retrospective accounts given by people in various circumstances who have succeeded against the odds. As a consequence, within the UK a planned form of youth mentoring has underpinned several interventions targeting 'socially excluded' young people (Philip, 2000).

However, youth mentoring remains too loosely defined, under-evaluated and poorly understood. The focus of existing literature on mentoring is on the 'doing' of mentoring as professional practice (Skinner and Fleming, 1999). Until recently much of the evaluation of such projects was carried out internally and was driven by a need to secure funding and to demonstrate 'success' in very narrow terms. As a result there has been a neglect of critical reflection on the concept.

Conceptualising mentoring within the UK

The term has also evoked highly partisan reactions (National Youth Agency, 1999). Many planned mentoring interventions, particularly in the USA, are based on 'taken for granted' assumptions about young people as being in deficit and as highly individualised actors in need of 'rescue' from their families, their peer groups or their communities (Herrera *et al.*, 2000). The North American experience of mentoring has been highly influential in the development of UK interventions and theorising of mentoring. Philip (2003) has pointed out elsewhere the dominance of developmental paradigms about youth in American work, which neglects new understandings of the diversity of youth and the new sociology of childhood.

Mentoring has become a major element of recent UK government policy directed towards young people and their families, with a heavy focus on young people defined as socially excluded. For example, in England, mentoring is a component of the national Connexions Service, the New Deal and various crime reduction strategies. In Scotland the new Scottish Parliament has made a renewed commitment to the development of mentoring programmes under the heading of 'supporting stronger and safer communities for children and young people' (Scottish Executive, 2003). However as the concept has become increasingly popular, gaps in knowledge about the benefits of the concept have become more evident (Colley, 2001).

A small body of work has begun to analyse the underpinnings of mentoring interventions from more critical perspectives (Philip, 1997). The main body of this work lies in theoretical and applied research, which is largely based on assumptions that young people are themselves active participants in the processes (Shucksmith and

Hendry, 1998). In this way it has taken a very different direction to the more developmentally-focused North American work on youth mentoring.

Colley, for example (2003), has explored mentoring within UK post-compulsory training and education programmes which targeted 'disaffected' young people. She has usefully identified the dominant model within these schemes as one of 'engagement mentoring', which she suggests privileges the agendas of institutions rather than young people in attempts to integrate them into the labour market. Within the new Connexions Service and the New Deal, mentors work with young people with a remit to guide them into appropriate training and careers. Colley argued cogently that such mentoring interventions are predicated on adjusting attitudes, behaviour and beliefs about employability. This is done at the expense of attention to structural inequalities and constraints that may themselves frame the experience of the young person. Mentors aim to develop 'quasi-parental' bonds between themselves and the young person as a means of developing a 'holistic approach' to their needs. However Colley suggested that the young person has little control over this despite being the focus of the intervention, since the intervention is essentially institutionally driven towards fostering employability. She highlighted how tensions arose when some young people and, more occasionally, their mentors subverted this agenda by forming strong relationships based on concerns that were significant to the young people but that lay beyond this narrow remit. Managers of the schemes tended to view these episodes as 'failures'. Moreover since mentoring within this scheme was based on the young person's employability, the relationship ended when they left the scheme. Colley concluded that this model of mentoring is tied to a narrow notion of employability, and suffers tight timescales, compulsion and a lack of flexibility, all of which are at odds with themes of mentoring as a

reciprocal and negotiated relationship. This led Colley to conclude that 'engagement mentoring' fragments the experiences of the young person and that the claim to be a 'holistic' intervention is false.

Forrest (2002) explored dimensions of mentoring from the perspective of adult volunteer befrienders. Within befriending projects, young people are matched with an adult with the aim of providing respite, alternative role models and opportunities to meet with an unrelated adult to take part in joint leisure activities. Within some befriending relationships a mentoring element can develop. Forrest examined how befrienders in one project described their relationships with young people as producing a form of social capital for them through doing 'emotion work'. Emotion work, as she described it, provided support and nurturing, which often goes unnoticed. She presented an optimistic conclusion about the benefits by suggesting that befriending should be viewed as a 'loaned and somewhat limited form of friendship' with the caveat that this 'new form of intimacy can be of a particularly bounded, conditional and unequal nature'.

Clayden and Stein (2002) recently completed a study of mentoring for care leavers in which they examined outcomes for mentors and young people over a 6- and 12-month period. The study drew on data from 22 projects, involving stakeholders, mentors and young people. Their findings demonstrated that young people were generally positive about involvement with mentors, believing that they provided a range of support, and a 'listening ear'. They pointed out that such an intervention can offer practical and emotional support within a safe and flexible climate to a particularly vulnerable section of the youth population who are often lacking in social relationships.

Philip and Hendry defined informal mentoring as a relationship that developed out of an existing friendship or naturally occurring relationship and that was characterised as providing support, guidance and challenge to the young person. From their study of informal mentoring, Philip and Hendry (1996) devised a typology of mentoring as a means of theorising the concept more coherently. Within the typology, five mentoring styles were evident and these are briefly described below:

1 'Classic' mentoring consists of a one-to-one relationship between an adult and a young person where the older, experienced mentor provides support, advice and challenge. Support may be offered, for instance, through working on a shared interest or hobby, where the adult provides a role model and gives recognition to the mentee as a 'special' person.

2 By contrast, 'individual–team' mentoring takes place where a group looks to an individual or small number of individuals for support, advice and challenge. This is most often, though not always, demonstrated in specialised youth work settings such as girls' groups. Sometimes it was mentioned by young people without reference to any 'organised' youth provision. The mentor is described as having both respect and understanding for the peer group and is not necessarily much older than the group members but may be recognised as having valid previous experience, which is seen as reliable and relevant.

3 'Friend-to-friend' mentoring often provides a 'safety net', especially for some young people who are mistrustful of adults. In some instances it provides a testing ground for disclosure of sensitive information, or a setting where values and beliefs can be rehearsed 'safely' prior to some form of action being taken. This type of mentoring relationship was most often cited within pairings of young women who were 'best friends' and who were also involved in a wider set of overlapping friendships.

4 Within 'peer group' mentoring, an ordinary friendship group will adopt a mentoring role at specific times. Such mentoring often occurs when a group of same-age friends or acquaintances share a common issue such as drug misuse and usually takes place within a specific social context. The peer group acts as an arbiter or a resource in terms of the appropriate strategies to adopt in certain social settings such as nightclubs, events, and stages of relationships with potential partners.

5 Finally, 'long-term relationship' mentoring with 'risk taking' adults. This style is similar to 'classic' mentoring in many respects, but is distinctive in that it is often a relationship between a young person and a mentor who has had a history of rebellion and of challenging authority and who is perceived by the young person as resisting adult definitions of the social world. Often these are young adults who are known from early childhood.

The new UK work on mentoring, described above, suggests a need to extend the typology to embrace the practice developments for planned mentoring within the UK (Colley, 2003). Such a model could take account of, for example, engagement mentoring, within which there is a combination of voluntary and paid staff and where there is an element of compulsion to the intervention. It could also more adequately take account of the spectrum of befriending relationships that includes a mentoring component, and also of youth work mentoring which may link more closely to informal mentoring as identified above (Millburn *et al.*, 2003). This could also yield insights into the wider context within which planned mentoring takes place.

The study reported here uses a definition of mentoring as:

> *... a process within a relationship or set of relationships which embodies elements of trust, reciprocity, challenge, support and control and which has the potential to empower the partners.*
> (Philip, 1997)

Following this, planned mentoring can be described as a set of processes within which a relationship is introduced purposefully, with the aim of fostering a meaningful relationship between a young person and a significant adult.

Chapter 2 outlines the parameters, aims and methods of this study. Background sketches of the projects are given in Chapter 3 and brief profiles of three participants make up Chapter 4. In Chapter 5, findings from the work with young people are described and analysed. Chapter 6 then examines findings from interviews with mentors, and the final chapter draws together conclusions from the study and highlights key implications of the findings.

2 The current study

It is important to indicate at the outset that this study is not a description of the work of the three projects studied or a straightforward evaluation of effectiveness, but rather an account given principally through the eyes of young people, of their experiences of mentoring within these settings. To a lesser extent, accounts given by mentors, parents and carers and stakeholders are also discussed.

The key themes that underpin this study include first, an examination of whether differences exist between planned mentoring approaches that take place as a paid activity (e.g. within the remit of a key worker or youth worker), and planned mentoring that is undertaken by volunteers, matched by a professional co-ordinator. Much of the emphasis in studies of mentoring to date has been on volunteer mentors who are recruited through community appeals or volunteer networks. However it is clear that mentoring takes place with professionals and semi-professionals, particularly in youth work settings. There may be valuable lessons from these different experiences and the frameworks on which mentoring is based. Secondly, it is important to understand the ways in which young people interpret planned mentoring processes in relation to other relationships within their existing social networks and other professional interventions. This could enhance knowledge about how best to time and target mentoring interventions. Finally, the ways in which young people's own diverse backgrounds and experiences interact with mentoring processes is an important aspect that has been neglected to date and that is addressed in this study.

Aims and methods of the research

The aims identified at the outset of the study were to:

- undertake an analysis of how planned mentoring interventions were perceived by a sample of vulnerable young people who have experienced risk

- examine the differences between planned mentoring interventions which are based on a voluntary commitment by the mentor and those which form an element of a paid professional remit

- compare approaches to mentoring within two projects, taking account of the different needs of groups of vulnerable young people within the 15–17-year age group, different timescales and geographical location

- investigate the organisational structures that best support planned mentoring interventions

- explore how perceptions held by young people inform the development of mentoring interventions

- examine how mentors and befrienders perceive their role within the different settings.

From these, the specific research questions below were developed:

- In what circumstances do relationships with key workers or befrienders become mentoring relationships? In which ways are such relationships significant over time to the participants in this study?

- How do such relationships develop and what are the underlying processes at work?

- How do young people interpret planned mentoring relationships as opposed to informal relationships within their existing social networks?

- How do the accounts of mentors compare with the perceptions of young people who have been mentored?

Methods and sampling

The methods used in the study were ethnographic and qualitative, using observation, individual and group interviews. The data gathering strategy involved:

- A literature review.

- Analysis of documentary evidence.

- Ethnographic observation of relationships between young people and mentors in the three chosen settings.

- Two phases of individual interviews approximately one year apart with young people currently involved in mentoring relationships. In the first round, 18 young people between 13 and 17 years of age, participated in interviews. Of these, 11 were young women and 7 were young men and the average age was 15. Fifteen repeat interviews took place in the second round with nine young women and six young men. In this second round, the average age was 16.

- Interviews with young people who were previously involved in the schemes. Fourteen interviews took place with young people previously involved in the schemes. The average age was 18 and equal numbers of men and women participated. A further three focus group interviews were held with young people who were previously involved with the befriending project.

- Interviews with mentors, key informants and parents/carers. Fifteen interviews were undertaken with mentors and a further ten with key informants from managing bodies, partner organisations, professionals, parents and carers of young people participating in the schemes. Seven parents and carers were also interviewed.

Following on from the initial ethnographic work with the projects, a purposive sample was selected for interview from within each project to reflect a balance of gender and representation of young people from different backgrounds. Attempts to recruit participants from minority ethnic groups were largely unsuccessful. This principally reflects the low numbers of people from minority ethnic groups in the wider population of the north of Scotland but may also suggest the existence of barriers to the use of the projects amongst some groups in the area. Efforts to include young people with different levels of ability were more successful.

Participants described in this report were defined as being vulnerable in some key respect. However, the reasons given for this definition were diverse and reflect the complexity of the notion of 'vulnerability' noted by Furlong and Cartmel (1997). Most, although not all, had grown up in poverty. Many had missed substantial periods of school. Most had experienced family breakdown and a range of caring relationships including foster care. A number had experience of long-term family illness and this ranged from degenerative illnesses to addiction to a range of substances. Some had experienced family disability and a substantial number themselves experienced poor physical or mental health. A number indicated that they had been abused and some had received or were still having treatment for substance misuse.

Ethnographic work

Activities to create the ethnography included the following, all of which have been recorded either by note-taking or by audio-tape recording where this was appropriate and permission was given by participants:

- production of information leaflets and background information (All sites)

- initial meetings with projects (All sites)

- initial meetings with participants (All sites)

- attendance at training events and support meetings (Befriending)

- attendance at team meetings (Education and Housing)

- attendance at AGMs, board meetings (Befriending)

- observation based on 'hanging around' (Education and Housing)

- informal chats and sitting in with staff and volunteers (All sites)

- home visits (Befriending)

- attendance at outings and activities (All sites)

- participation in group activities (All sites)

- planned events around the research, e.g. group sessions based around a meal.

Interviews

A framework for interviews was piloted with young people and professionals prior to undertaking the first round of interviews. In addition to background data about the young person, the framework was used to initiate discussion on relationships and social networks. In order to encourage participation and to create a relaxed setting, a range of games and vignettes was designed. In addition, a 'spider's web' was constructed on which social relationships could be described and mapped in discussion with the researcher.

All interviews were taped with the permission of participants. At the end of the first interview, participants received a small gratuity of £10 in recognition of their time and commitment and as an encouragement to participate in a second round of interviews. They received a further gratuity of £25 at the end of the second interview. In the reporting of this work, all participants have been given pseudonyms.

A semi-structured format was used for interviews with professionals. This was also piloted and subsequently adjusted in the light of discussion within the research team and following feedback from participants.

In total, 33 individual interviews took place over rounds 1 and 2 with young people who were matched to key workers or befrienders divided between the projects. An additional 24 retrospective interviews were undertaken with young people who had previously been involved but had dropped out, been excluded or left the projects. The original intention had been to carry out group interviews with this sample, but this was only possible with three groups from the befriending project. Recruiting groups from the other projects proved very difficult owing to the scattered nature of the sample. For this reason the project team decided to focus on individual interviews for the retrospective work with the education and housing projects. Fifteen individual interviews took place with mentors in all the projects. A further ten interviews were undertaken with key informants, which included individuals from referring agencies, management groups and other service providers. Finally seven interviews took place with parents or carers.

3 Background to the projects

Covesea Intensive Housing Project

This project is nested within a national voluntary organisation, Aberlour Childcare Trust, which works with vulnerable young people. The project is based in a market town in the north-east of Scotland. This is a small district which until recently depended heavily on farming, fishing and forestry industries, all of which are now in decline. The local economy is reliant on two large air force bases, service industries and to a smaller extent, tourism and distilling. It is a relatively prosperous area with a high volume of in-migration, mainly of elderly people, but it has pockets of unemployment and a degree of rural poverty. As a result it qualifies for EC rural development funding and regeneration funding. Youth unemployment has always been high and at the time of the study considerable media attention was focused on crime among young people in the area. The latest census figures recorded increases in the numbers of minority ethnic groups living in the area but the proportion remains at less than 1 per cent.

The project takes a 'person centred' approach, within which youth mentoring has a prominent part. It is one element of a partnership which links the voluntary agency with the local authority housing and social work departments, youth crime teams and other voluntary agencies with an interest in working with vulnerable young people. This particular form of the project emerged from previous work with young people in the '16–18 Initiative' which had been funded by the National Lotteries Board for three years (Forrest, 1999). The previous project had not offered accommodation and, since housing presented a major issue for many in the target group, the current project was designed to fill this gap.

Within the project, tenancies and training are offered to young people who have experienced homelessness or vulnerability. Although the project aims to cater for 16–25 year olds, allocations are generally in the 16–18 age group. Young people arrived at the project through a range of routes: many were in temporary accommodation; some had tenancies which they could not sustain; some had been in care; some had problems rooted in misuse of alcohol or other substances; some had been thrown out by parents; some had mental health problems, learning difficulties or behavioural problems; many had experienced abuse. The majority of those interviewed were previously known to the social work department and caring agencies in the area.

Assessments are made by the young person's officer within the local authority and places are then allocated by the management group. The project caters for six tenants, with an additional group of up to ten trainees who attend on a part-time (non-residential) basis for the training element. The project is staffed by care workers on a shift system which offers 24-hour support to the tenants. Funding is wholly through transitional housing benefit, with capital costs met by the Social Inclusion Partnership (SIP), and management by the voluntary organisation. Mentoring within the project is undertaken by paid key workers, some of whom are also responsible for assessing whether young people should continue their tenancy. Moving on from the project is negotiated with staff through a series of reviews and assessments. A number of young people were evicted from the project within the first six months of the beginning of the study, after a serious 'trashing' of the premises which led to a well publicised court case and jail sentences for some of the residents.

Young people are matched with a key worker by the co-ordinator, usually in consultation with the worker. Although young people have no choice over the selection of their key worker, they are free to discuss issues with other members of staff. The staff adopt a team approach, in which information is shared about individual young people. Key workers may change in some circumstances and this can be negotiated with the young person. Key workers meet both informally and formally with the young person, take responsibility for helping them to make and keep appointments and generally oversee progress. Most young people appeared to be familiar with the key worker scheme before joining the project. Staff have a managerial role in supporting young people to move towards independent living and this is negotiated through a series of reviews.

Pinefield Education Project

This is an educational resource for young people in the 12–16 age group who have experienced difficulties at school. One worker described the project as 'the end of the line' for young people who had been excluded or who had opted out of formal education.

It is located in a purpose-built small unit on an industrial estate on the outskirts of the same market town where the housing project is situated. The project is funded by the local authority and was managed by Aberlour Childcare Trust as part of a larger youth project until April 2003 when the Education Department of the local authority took over. A co-ordinator and teacher are employed on a full-time basis with two part-time teachers. The part-time teachers have no key worker responsibilities, but in other respects are team members. Two full-time and two part-time project workers make up the team, all with key worker roles. Some young people have key workers within the project but also receive support from youth workers from other teams within the umbrella project such as the criminal justice team, the community-based team and the moving on team. Some also have support from other agencies in the district.

Referrals are made to the project by social work, criminal justice, schools and occasionally parents. The project aims to work with the young person to develop a curriculum tailored to individual needs and to offer a mix of academic and vocational subjects. English and Mathematics are compulsory subjects but otherwise the curriculum is negotiated. Most of the work is on a one-to-one basis, but group activities also take place. A number of young people combine attendance at the project with work experience, college courses or sessions within schools. Attendance at the centre varies from two months to three years, depending on the needs of the young people.

A high staff/young person ratio is in place. Some workers are qualified in social work, community education or related fields and others are semi-professional, recruited for their abilities to work with and empathise with the needs of the target group. During the course of the study, encouragement was given to these workers to gain a professional qualification.

Key workers meet both formally and informally with young people, usually seeing them on a day-to-day basis within the project, often collecting them and transporting them to the project. In addition, they may jointly take part in practical work, such as going to buy food and preparing meals at the project. The key worker often acts as an informal advocate with GPs, psychological services, dentists and other agencies. This was especially evident in relation to negotiating psychological and health services. A pragmatic approach is taken to working with young people as the co-ordinator explained:

if they don't want to be there then they won't learn or they won't turn up, both of which are counterproductive. So we try to work around that as far as possible and this means that often it is 1:1 or very small groups.

Dundee Youth-Link Befriending Project

The befriending project offers a service for young people aged 5 to 18 through one-to-one befriending and group work in Dundee. Funding of the organisation comes from the local authority, charitable trusts, and fund-raising. Funding is a continuing issue for the project. The project was established in 1981 and is therefore one of the longest established befriending projects in Scotland.

Dundee, situated in the east of Scotland with a population of over 140,000, is a city where traditional industries are in decline. Statistics indicate below average educational attainment level for school-leavers, high levels of unemployment and heavy reliance on income support, high numbers of single parent households and below average household income. Numbers of teenage pregnancies and death rates from cancer are above average for Scotland. It has a diverse, but small minority ethnic population. The three most numerous groups are people from Pakistan, India and China. It is estimated that there are around 1,000 young people living in the city from a minority ethnic background.

The project employs four paid staff who support a group of volunteers to carry out befriending. The manager, development worker and administrator are full time and the public relations worker is employed for ten hours per week. Approximately 50 volunteers are trained, with 40 currently matched with young people. The majority of referrals are made by the social work department of the local authority with the rest from health visitors, Home School Support Service, parents, clinical psychologists and voluntary sector agencies concerned with child welfare or combating violence against women and families. At one point in the course of the study 65 young people were on the waiting list as referrals. Generally, the referral is discussed with the young person. Owing to the time lapse between being referred and matched this discussion is sometimes delayed until a suitable volunteer has been allocated.

After a young person is matched with a volunteer, the relationship is continually negotiated with the young person. The intervention is therefore a voluntary one on the part of the young person and the volunteer, so that at any point the young person can decide not to continue the relationship. Meetings between the partners take place weekly or fortnightly and they participate in a range of activities which are chosen to reflect the interests of the young person.

Group activities are also organised by the project and these may be open to young people who are not currently matched with a befriender. Thus one group is targeted at young people whose lives are in some way affected by a disability or long-term illness in the home. This group is facilitated by a paid worker supported by volunteers. A girls' group and a newsletter group, which were running at the beginning of the study, have since stopped meeting.

Summary

It is clear from these brief descriptions that critical differences exist between the structure of the housing, education and befriending projects. Both the housing and education projects employ paid key workers, whereas the befriending project comprises a large group of volunteers who are managed by a small team of paid staff. Further, the funding arrangements of the housing and education projects are fairly generous, whereas the befriending project receives minimal core funding and is constantly faced with the need to fund-raise. Within the housing and education projects, young people and key workers mix on a daily basis, whereas within the befriending project contact is limited to pre-organised weekly to fortnightly meetings. Finally, within the housing project and education projects, key workers had responsibilities to manage tenancies and behaviour, while befrienders had no other responsibilities. This was particularly the case for key workers within the housing project in their attempts to ensure young people complied with police curfews. Thus the mentoring role appeared to be more constrained for the key workers.

4 Introducing some young people

In this chapter, three case studies of individuals are presented. They are included here to give a more rounded and holistic view of the lives of these vulnerable young people. Each project – befriending, housing and education – provides one case study.

Profile 1: Teresa (housing project)

Teresa's slight build made her seem much younger than her real age of 16 at the first interview. At this point, she had been a tenant of a flat within the housing project for three months.

Teresa had lived with her mum and brothers in different places within the district until she left home. In the first round, she stated forcefully that she disliked her father and avoided him. By the second round they were in regular contact. Her relationship with her mother was important to her and she felt close to her.

Her first tenancy after leaving home failed: she had found it difficult and lonely living on her own and had developed a serious problem with alcohol. She described how her flat became a centre for 'druggies, alcoholics and jail people' and she became so powerless that she had felt she was in physical danger. Finally, a worker from the housing project had physically taken her away and helped her to move into the project.

At the first interview, Teresa emphasised how much she liked her project flat and felt settled. An important aspect was that 'I can shut the door and only let people in if I want to'. The flat was very tidy, furnished simply and decorated with photographs and cards from her family. She was optimistic about the future and it was clear that she was popular with staff and other residents. Her relationship with her boyfriend, also a resident at this stage, was on and off but she hoped it would continue. Teresa had recently returned to school with the encouragement of her key worker. She hoped to gain enough passes to help her train for a

career as a drug and alcohol counsellor. She believed her own experiences and those of family and former boyfriends had given her insight into the problems facing substance misusers. The achievements of Joyce, the co-ordinator of the project, and the counselling skills used by Maria, a project worker, also influenced this ambition. Teresa had missed a lot of her course but hoped to catch up and to gain reasonable passes.

However, by the second round, she had left school, having failed all her exams and her confidence was at a low ebb. She still hoped to become a counsellor and planned to start a college course. By then Teresa had, very unwillingly, moved out of the project accommodation into her own tenancy and was living with her boyfriend who had been released from prison. This flat felt much less personal than her former flat and Teresa was clearly depressed.

Teresa had known some of the tenants and workers in the project before she moved in. In the first round she described herself as very close to Maria, Duncan and Joyce, three workers at the project. Teresa described Maria as:

> one of the workers here, I dunno, She is just like when you speak to her about your problems, she has always got a way to solve them, always, it's like [puts on a voice] 'it's not that bad, we can do this and we can do that' and she makes it seem a whole lot better.

Teresa made a distinction between the support she received from Maria and Duncan. She described Maria as more of a 'mummy figure' whereas she viewed Duncan as someone with whom she could 'test out' things about relationships as 'he is a bloke and blokes are all the same'. She also viewed Duncan as having experienced similar problems to her own. She claimed that she wouldn't swear in front of Maria, not because she felt Maria would be offended but because 'you have respect for your mum and dad and don't swear in front of them and that'. Teresa described the project co-ordinator, Joyce, as someone who had helped her sort out her life by accepting her:

> *Without her, I probably wouldn't be here and my life would probably still be a mess.*
> (Round 1 interview)

and

> *She put me somewhere safe and gave me the chance to sort my life out.*
> (Round 2 interview)

Teresa described her relationship with her key worker (Jill) in somewhat different terms from Duncan and Joyce. She was aware from the outset that the key worker had a say in the continuation of her tenancy and this made her slightly cautious. Her relationship with Jill had developed since then. When she got upset, as she sometimes did, Jill often took her away from the project to talk things over. When asked how her friends and family perceived Jill, Teresa struggled to describe her role:

> *Well, my friends most of them have been up here anyway and most of them have met Jill and they are all, oh she is so cool, she's magic an' a' that. But they don't really [understand] – it is … like a social worker, but she is not.*

By the second round the relationship was terminated as Jill had moved to another post in the agency, but they re-established contact when Teresa began work experience through the project.

Teresa was reluctant to 'move on again' from the project and had made the point that she 'wasn't ready' at several reviews. Partly this was because she was aware that the nature of the support would change and partly because of a fear of coping on her own. She wanted to maintain her links:

> *When we move out of here like there is going to be a community group that works with us. But like, Maria works there, she works here as relief or something.*

And then I can always come up here, we can come up here whenever we want so they can never get rid of me.

In the second round, she highlighted differences in the support she received from the community team compared with that of the housing workers. The community team focused on the practical skills of managing a tenancy, which included budgeting, homemaking and shopping. They placed less emphasis on emotional or mentoring support. Several workers were involved and she felt this made the relationships less personalised. Her support had tapered from daily contact to twice weekly since she had shown that she was coping. When she first moved into her flat, she returned to the project most evenings, explaining that she found it hard to adapt to the lack of company. Although she was happy living with David, her boyfriend, they had their ups and downs and overall she regretted leaving the project, feeling that 'it was too early for me'.

Profile 2: Sara (education project)

At the first interview, Sara was 15 and had been attending the project for several months. Initially she had continued for part of the week in mainstream schooling but this arrangement had broken down and she described herself as full time at the project. Sara was underweight, with immaculate hair and makeup and was very anxious. She explained that she was tense about moving in with a new set of foster parents later that day. By the second interview, she was living happily with these foster parents. She had gained some standard grades and was doing a part-time course on hair and beauty at the further education college. Although she found college 'difficult', she enjoyed parts of it, was getting additional study support and was pleased that she was 'sticking it out'. Sara was more confident and took a relaxed and thoughtful approach to this second interview.

Her parents divorced when Sara was a baby. She later made contact with her father, but described this as a 'disaster', finding him violent and misusing drugs. Her mother had remarried and she described her stepfather as a key figure who had brought her up since she was three years old. When she was ten, however, her mother left her stepfather, taking the children, though Sara subsequently lived with him at different periods. In the second interview, she stated that living with him was not an option as they were too likely to argue, but they continued to meet weekly.

Sara claimed that she had taken on a lot of responsibility for her younger sister since her mum had difficulties in coping. She felt that this had contributed to her problems at school. She also believed her mother was a bad influence over her and unable to set boundaries. Nevertheless even when she was not in contact with her mother, she described her as the person to whom she felt closest, stating:

My mum, even though we are not speaking. She's always been the closest.

In the second interview, she described her feelings about this estrangement from her mother:

I was really upset that she didn't want to speak to me especially during the Christmas time because she never spoke on Christmas Day or anything so … it was like I was hurt.
(Round 2 interview)

She felt that all the family disruption was resulting in a problem with 'attachment'. While at primary school she had begun to see a range of professionals, including a psychiatrist, and this had continued during her teenage years.

Sara described herself as loud and abusive, as having a problem with alcohol, as having been abused and as anxious about her body. She also felt that she had been 'taken advantage of' and bullied in the past. She had also developed a reputation for fighting, partly because she had done kick boxing

but also because she had difficulties in managing her anger and in dealing with relationships. This led her to say her hair was the only thing she liked about her self. She had her first 'serious' relationship at 14 years of age and this was followed by some 'disastrous sexual experiences'.

By the second interview she had managed to 'stay out of trouble', had an improved relationship with her mother, had made some new friends and was on the way to a hairdressing career.

In the first interview, Sara described the staff group at the education project as an important source of support and challenge and the project itself as a safe and friendly environment. Although she felt that they did not 'judge' her, the staff seemed to know all about her and her activities, and this freed her up to talk about her problems. Her key worker was a male worker who she described as important in the first round, having introduced her to the project and made her feel part of the organisation. At the second interview, however, she expressed some bitterness about what she described as rejection by the project and by her key worker, when she had moved on from the project. Her account of her first day at college illustrated the tensions of this kind of relationship. Sara and her friend, who was also starting a course, had met the worker for breakfast. She was very worried that her past would set people against her at college and meeting up with her key worker gave her 'a good feeling' of support. When the worker didn't turn up the following day Sara was so angry that she telephoned him and swore at him. Her friend gave up college and this isolated Sara further. However she made some new friends and negotiated learning support for herself at the college. She still believed that the ending of the relationship was too abrupt.

Sara contrasted this experience with her continuing relationship with Pilar, a worker based at the sister project to the education project and sited next door. Sara described Pilar as helping her to deal with family issues and school problems in the two years prior to joining the project. Sara admired Pilar for being able to cope with 'so many teenagers in her life' and described her as being 'like a mother to me'. Pilar was her first contact if she was in difficulty. Central to this was Pilar's respect of her privacy:

Well I know Pilar is very confidential and if I don't want her to tell my mum or anything or anybody else then I know that she won't.

In both interviews, Sara constantly compared Pilar to her mother, often suggesting that Pilar provided the support that her mother was unable to offer. She met her at the project and also spent 'individual time' with her. Sara claimed that Pilar had agreed that Sara could phone her any time and although she had not taken up this offer she interpreted this as a sign that the relationship went beyond professional boundaries.

Sara also described how Pilar helped her to deal with problems that her mother ignored, including a brief period of notoriety when she was the subject of tabloid headlines. Again she held her mother responsible for failing to set boundaries for her:

she should have been there to say no you can't go out and get drunk. I mean it is okay to have a few drinks and that. But by that time we had fallen out and I had just gone wild. Cos she wasnae there to comfort me or anything.

At the second interview she described herself as no longer reliant on the education project, and mused that she had distanced herself from Pilar:

S: I don't know, it's weird me and Pilar get on but we are not keen ... we are not close, close because that is the thing you can't be too close. It would hurt if they left or anything ... If I looked on them as one of my family or anything, you can't do that.

Researcher: Are there times when you have ever felt you depended on a worker?

S: Aye I have ... Pilar ... When my mum wasn't speaking to me ... I was really hurting and I depended on the project then ... I could handle it now. I wouldn't worry if she stopped speaking to me because I know she would start speaking to me again because she can't stay away from me. I am her daughter for fucks sake!

In addition to Pilar, Sara also spent time with a woman worker in the education project, describing her as having helped her to develop ways of getting on better with other participants at the project and as someone with whom she could have a 'good laugh'. In a later interview, the worker described how she had negotiated boundaries with Sara for when they went out together in the town. She had felt that Sara's initially outrageous behaviour had 'been a nightmare' and had been a barrier to her being taken seriously by others. She had raised the issue using humour by replaying a scene that Sara had made and this appeared to have been successful:

And it has taken a long time for her to see that that wasn't normal that this is not how you behave when you are out and about ... so I used to show her up rotten. Because she did it to me and I know it sounds cruel but ... it was the only way that I could be comfortable ... to take her down the street.

It was clear that 'having a laugh' with a worker who was herself prepared to look ridiculous, had achieved a lot. It was also evident that this strategy could have backfired if a degree of trust hadn't been built up between the worker and the young person. Although Sara's contact with this worker was very occasional by the second round of interviews, she continued to regard her as a significant influence.

At school, Sara had felt that staff had no time for pupils like herself who 'weren't perfect'. She felt they made little attempt to help her or to recognise her attempts to deal with her problems. Sara was quick to draw distinctions between teachers in mainstream schools and those at the education project who had welcomed her, awakened her interest, and taken her seriously:

> you do the stuff that you are meant to do, but they do it in a different way, so you're doing it more because you want to.

Profile 3: Lorna (befriending project)

Lorna was 14 at the first interview and living with her foster parent, Angela, who had her own family. She was unhappy living with Angela as she felt excluded from this family group and believed that she was treated differently from the other children. She had been very happy with her first set of foster carers who had cared for her over six years. By the second interview, she was with her third set of foster parents, having spent a short period living with an older sister between placements. Although she was not allowed to live with her mother, she reported at the first interview that they saw each other daily. However by the second round of interviews, contact had lessened, and Lorna claimed this was because her mum was recovering from problems with alcohol. She felt that her mum was envious that her carers were in a position to provide Lorna with something she was unable to give.

Lorna was the youngest of a family of four sisters and a brother. She barely remembered her father and had no desire to meet up with him. All her siblings were in care at some point.

Lorna was matched with Brenda as a befriender for a year, a relationship that ended when Brenda left to go travelling around the world. Her first impression of Brenda was shock at her 'knitted tights' and how different she was in appearance from Lorna. However, when they spoke to each other she felt that Brenda was really cool and genuine and immediately felt at ease with her. She described Brenda as someone 'who was interested in *me*' and that she had the right, as did her foster

carer, to put her in her place if Lorna was out of order. Above all she could have a laugh and talk about anything, in the knowledge that Brenda would help her think through the consequences of her actions. In this respect, she identified similarities between Brenda and one of her previous foster parents, William. She felt the relationship with Brenda was based on respect and more like a sister relationship in which any issue could be discussed.

She hadn't really understood what befriending was about at the outset and had asked 'if it was about going places', an option that she liked. However her experience was more about 'discussing things and problems' than outings. She expressed sadness that the relationship had ended and she hoped that should Brenda return to the area, they would link up again. By the second round she reported that, in the absence of Brenda, she discussed personal issues with her best friend (Sonia), her foster carer or her new social worker. She had known Sonia since they were babies when they had lived round the corner from each other. She believed that this long-term link was important; although their friendship had faded in the later years of primary school it was renewed in secondary school. She described it as a mutually supportive relationship in that they had both 'been there for each other' through difficult experiences.

In the first round, Lorna identified her previous carers, William and Catriona, as key supports and described how she planned to sustain contact after moving out. She felt particularly close to William and confided in him, seeing him as a father figure for whom she was special. She described how 'we used to go everywhere together' and how he often bought her presents, which irritated Catriona who was stricter. She gave the example of William secretly buying her a bus pass when Catriona had threatened that if she lost another one, she would not get a replacement. Lorna felt that William's willingness to put himself out for her and to knowingly risk the wrath of Catriona, strengthened their relationship. Throughout the first interview she returned to this theme, describing herself as 'gutted' when she moved out.

She never felt comfortable with her next foster carer and her family. However, by the second interview, she attributed her happiness to her latest carer. This latest carer had previously been her respite carer. Her opinion of William and Catriona had also changed dramatically since she had found a report they had written about her. She felt that this report was very unfair and showed they had a very different perception of her than she had believed.

She expressed mixed views about social workers, having got on well with her first social worker. However when she had tried to discuss a concern with her next social worker, he had just 'laughed at her' which she found very upsetting. Following this she rejected him as a source of support despite his encouragement to confide in him. Her current social worker was a woman that she felt would be more likely to advocate on her behalf:

> *... think she is just more genuine, and I think it is maybe because she is a woman that I speak to her more. And I think that she is truly, she really does care about me and my welfare, you know what I*

mean and what happens to us, whereas, Paul, just, well, I think he did in a way, I think he had a lot on his plate with work and that, so ...

She didn't see teachers in general as helpful to her, fearing staffroom gossip about her being in care. She qualified this with an anecdote about one teacher who she felt had been supportive to her without being patronising. But in the second round she reported on an incident where she thought the teacher had unjustly criticised her friend, giving this as an illustration of how teachers often undermined pupils. She felt strongly that teachers were often disrespectful of young people and their capabilities.

Lorna clearly spent a lot of time trying to make sense of her family relationships and the issues that she confronted. She came across as someone who was likeable, warm and friendly but also as able to make the best of situations in which she found herself. Despite all the disruption she had experienced, she focused on positive experiences with adults. This was evident in her view of social workers and teachers as having 'a lot on their plates' and her own resistance to replacement adults in her life. She described Brenda as engaging with her as a person and believed that part of the value was that Brenda also claimed to benefit from the relationship.

5 Findings: the views of young people

The findings are considered in relation to four research questions:

- In what circumstances do relationships with key workers or befrienders become mentoring relationships?

- How do such relationships develop and what are the underlying processes at work?

- How do young people interpret planned mentoring relationships, as opposed to informal relationships, within their existing social networks?

- How do the accounts of mentors relate to the perceptions of young people who have been mentored?

Finally, we relate these findings to the original typology of mentoring outlined in Chapter 1 and explore its relevance in theorising planned mentoring processes.

In what circumstances do relationships with key workers or befrienders become mentoring relationships?

In this section we explore young people's views of meaningful relationships with key workers and befrienders. We then examine to what extent these could be described as mentoring.

Individual mentoring

An important component of the work of the three projects was one-to-one work with young people. Within the befriending project the focus was on the development of a one-to-one relationship between a young person and a volunteer. Within the education and housing projects such relationships existed within a wider group environment. A number of young people clearly preferred individual attention. For Rory, this was an important factor in his decision to get involved in the befriending project:

R: … I don't like going out with large groups of people all the time. I am more a home person. And so I just agreed to try it out and then it was ok so it kind of worked … had a feeling that it was a kind of a group thing … where you went round in a big group and I don't know, you went to … parks on picnics and things. I don't know, I didn't think it was just one on one going to the cinema.

Researcher: Right, and do you prefer it being one on one, or …

R: Yeah, I am not really the multi-social person.
(Befriending)

Within the education project, the mix of individual and group work with a range of staff held strong appeal:

Aye like at the project, there is always stuff to do, like when you go up there, there is always like … even if your key worker has to nip away or that, like there is always folk up there to sit and speak to. At [another agency] I don't know anyone either. It's like really boring because down there you just go and sit in an office and just sit and speak to your key worker, like one to one. But like up [there] you get to like speak to other folk and I know other folk that go there.
(Education)

Within the education project, some tensions existed between key workers' managerial responsibilities for reviewing the progress of young people and their mentoring role. For example, although young people were consulted over the content of reports that staff wrote for social workers, the children's hearing system and for schools, scope existed for disagreement. This tension often emerged when reports were compiled to inform decisions by the agency and others about the continued involvement of young people at the project.

A positive image of the young person

Young people who reported positive mentoring relationships, highlighted the importance of the mentor accepting them on their own terms. Thus Diana identified her befriender as the first person she had met who had taken a positive approach to her hyperactivity:

> *It wasn't confidence that made me want a befriender, it was because I needed somebody active and Susan was active. Like we went canoeing, we went to karate and stuff like that, we went to the cinema.*
> (Befriending)

Within the housing project, Lisa valued how the mentor had recognised her as capable of helping out, being trusted and viewed as worthy of having a reciprocal relationship:

> *She owns a pub and she used to let me go up and do a couple of hours waitressing and that for her as well to get like a wee bit of money as well.*
> (Housing)

Shared backgrounds and contexts

For some young people a shared understanding gained through similar life experiences with their key worker/befriender led them to define a relationship as significant. Teresa (Profile 1), for example, felt embarrassed about discussing some areas of her life with her key worker and felt more able to explore these with another carer in the project who made connections between her experiences and his own past. Speaking about this worker, she said:

> *I know a lot about Duncan. Duncan has spoken to me a lot about his past. Because I was upset one night and he told me a lot about his past. That made me cry.*
> (Housing)

Teresa explained that this did not mean her key worker did not provide her with mentoring support, but that she would be selective about what she discussed with her. By the second round, Teresa had sporadic contact with the key worker but still phoned Duncan regularly to discuss problems. She continued to receive support from the project but no longer described this as mentoring, preferring to rely on Duncan, her boyfriend and her best friend. In this way she identified Duncan's support as disconnected from the project. Sara (Profile 2) observed that people who had not had problems themselves were often unable to understand the complexities of her life. For her, a mentor who had been in trouble as a young person was more likely both to empathise and to know when she was 'taking the piss' or trying to manipulate the situation. Thus, Sara suggested that within the education project, workers always seemed to 'see through her' and to know what she had 'really been up to':

> *They always knew what I got up to no matter what, they always knew honestly, they knew when you were lying. So that was about it.*
> (Education)

She claimed that this made it easier for her to be honest and to discuss what underlay her behaviour. Both Teresa and Sara talked about how they discussed issues with different professionals in their lives. For both, mentoring permitted them to drop their guard about their own behaviour and to seek support from people that they viewed as likely to understand their realities or to give informed advice.

In a similar vein, Norman described his social worker who was not attached to the project, as one of the constants in his life. Key to this was that she had remained with him through a number of moves in and out of care and important incidents. Nevertheless he stated that when he got into trouble he was less likely to talk to her first, since she was likely to 'give me a lecture' and adopt a quasi-parental stance. If he had still attended the education project, he would have looked to his key worker because:

... she would make me look at why I did it. She would make me face up to it.
(Education)

Many young people in the befriending project appeared to lead less chaotic lives than those involved in the housing and education projects. They were more likely to join the project because of family problems that impinged on them, for example a sibling with ADHD, parental alcohol or health problems or long-term illness. Thus, the focus of befriending was often on providing respite or time out. For example, Rory described himself as unsociable and isolated and, for him, befriending provided an opportunity to relax and enjoy activities with a companion who had similar interests. Although his befriender knew that his mother had a degenerative illness, this was not the subject of their conversations.

Rory defined the intervention as a mix of support through difficulties and as offering a social space:

Well I told my friend, because he was like, you get to go out on Saturday nights, what is it all about? Mm I don't know, it is just someone who just, if you need a friend, I don't know, if you have a family break up or something and you need to get connected with someone, you know, for fun. A chance to get out really because I didn't really get out much before.
(Befriending)

He drew some lines about what would be discussed with his befriender:

... say we had fall outs at home, I wouldn't talk to Stewart about that. I wouldn't want that information leaking out or anything, but say it is just a problem, like mm I don't know, having disagreements with any of my friends, or getting problems at school. Maybe I could talk to Stewart about that.
(Befriending)

However this view appeared to be related to his own strategies for dealing with difficult situations and less with not trusting his befriender.

Lorna gave a contrasting view on a befriending relationship that was based on a mutual respect by both partners and which 'gelled' from the outset:

I think it is [about] respecting her not about rules. That means that I know what Brenda wants and Brenda knows what I am expecting. That is better than setting rules ... befriending wasn't really about just going places, it was sort of discussing things and problems ... Brenda is like a friend, I don't really think of her just as a befriender, I think of her as a friend, you know, like a sister, you know, like somebody you could talk to, like somebody that way.
(Befriending)

Having a laugh

A sense of humour was frequently the key to developing and sustaining relationships as Eric's excerpt suggests:

It was great, yeah, it was really good to see him, so. Yeah, that was fantastic yeah, you know, he was one of the best befrienders that I have ever had basically, he was really funny, and somebody's personality makes a big difference, and his personality was just so good, mm, he was funny he was, mm, he was a laugh, he saw a good side of everything, he saw a funny side of everything basically, he was always optimistic, you know, he was never moody or pessimistic or anything like that, he was always, he was just always great fun to be with.
(Befriending)

This often allowed a young person to admit to going off the rails in some way. It covered a wide spectrum from sharing a joke, to recognition of a shared sense of humour and a shared capacity to laugh at their own actions. Participants often drew on examples of having a laugh to highlight differences between relationships with their mentors and other professionals. Having a laugh was therefore an important component of a trusting relationship and symbolised the reciprocity that many participants prized. In the following example, the mentor continued to play a significant part in Scott's life although contact with the agency had lessened by the second round of interviews:

He's funny, he listens … well like if I have had a fall out with somebody and like ken Ben he has been there ken … like because if I have a blow out, that's what I call it if I lose my temper, Ben will say 'Look just calm down', and that and he has helped me again to control myself so he has helped me in that way as well.
(Education)

Lorna drew a distinction between this kind of relationship and one where she felt that she was not sharing in the laugh, but where the social worker was laughing at her:

Yeah you couldnae say nothing or he would laugh and go [imitates pompous laugh] *that is quite funny. He used to complain to me, he would say, 'Lorna, I don't think you speak to me enough' and I would think 'It's because you laugh at us, what do you expect?' Because he had this accent and you just couldn't speak to him about anything and I was like that* [shrugs].
(Befriending)

Some young people described the backgrounds of some befrienders as a barrier, at least in the initial stages. Many befrienders were students or older parents whose own children had grown up and many lived in middle-class areas. The majority of young people lived in public housing and had parents who were unemployed or poorly paid. The social distance this conferred made it less likely that many befrienders would be regarded as confidants. Many befrienders were highly mobile, moving away or into education or full-time work. However the transient nature of some befrienders' lives sometimes opened up the potential of different worlds for a number of young people whose expectations until then were bounded by what Macdonald (Mason *et al.*, 2000) has called 'bounded socioscapes'.

In contrast to these befrienders, the semi-professional and professional workers in the housing and education projects often came from working class backgrounds, had experienced family break-up, and had unconventional backgrounds that they were prepared to discuss with the young people. This lent them an authority and a credibility in the eyes of many young people who perceived them as not only having survived similar problems to their own but also succeeding in a difficult area of work. This potential to become resilient adults, living 'normal' lives, was a key theme in the accounts of Teresa and Sara. The theme of professionals and semi-professionals getting closer to the young people than the volunteers was an unexpected finding, in that we had anticipated that the managerial aspects of paid workers' remits might make them less likely to be viewed as potential allies or advocates for their clients. One befriending match provided a clear contradiction to this: Catherine and Serena were from similar backgrounds and their relationship was very fluid, with less distinct boundaries and flexible agreements.

Localised and community based

In some ways, sharing a laugh symbolised a narrowing of the social distance between the mentor and the young person. Many of the mentors in the education and housing projects lived locally and had connections with the social and even family networks of the young people. Befrienders generally had less localised knowledge. This can be explained in part by the relatively rural area and the stable population compared with the more anonymous city setting of the befriending project. But it may have implications for the development of neighbourhood-based mentoring within larger centres of population.

Because befrienders had fewer connections with other social networks such as family and friends, building up a picture of the overall context was more problematic. However this was not always negative as the decontextualised aspect of befriending allowed young people to have some respite from their problems and to simply enjoy activities that they might not otherwise be able to try out. The co-ordinator of the befriending project, who had a long-term commitment to the project, had better access to localised knowledge and understanding of family networks and histories. This pivotal role of the co-ordinator became clearer in the second phase of interviews.

The education project focused on activities as well as formal education, and young people took part in the buying, preparation and organisation of daily meals at the project. These provided a setting where trivial and important issues could be discussed informally. Key workers spent a great deal of time transporting young people and doing a range of mundane as well as more focused tasks on an individual or a paired basis. Before Sara (Profile 2) went shopping with her key worker, agreements were made about language and behaviour, a process which involved both humour and straight talking. This contributed to a sense of reciprocity with the young person and the mentor working together. Young people often contrasted this with uncomfortable and formalised meetings with professionals 'sitting across the table'.

This informal working was also evident within the housing project where key workers again provided transport to appointments, joint buying of food for some meals, evenings out at bowling or skating, support at court hearings and seeking out training opportunities. Some young people in the housing project were subject to police curfews and the key worker had a legal requirement to notify police if these were broken even for a short time. Tensions were evident in situations where young people had broken the curfew and believed that a keyworker should have given more leeway.

Friendship and reciprocity

In all three projects, mentoring relationships were described as embodying elements of friendship. Rory described his befriending relationship as gradually becoming one of friendship, while Sara in her first interview described her mentor as 'like a friend … my youth worker'. Within the housing and education projects, key workers often drew on stories about their own risky pasts or by recounting anecdotes about their own lack of skills in particular areas. The informal nature of the relationship also encouraged young people to tell their stories, to examine how they could tackle the challenges that faced them and to rehearse new strategies with the worker.

Continuities

Within the education and housing projects, the person who made the initial contact sometimes became the mentor. John had joined the education project from the south of the country and attended the project for a year. He spoke about how joining the project had helped him become more confident and able to express his feelings. He attributed this to the welcoming climate and to how the worker who introduced him to the project, 'had a laugh with him' and made him feel comfortable in the group. He felt that they had developed a strong relationship but like many other young men who took part, he would be unlikely to discuss 'family stuff' with him. He brought other personal problems to this worker but emphasised that time was needed to develop this relationship. John felt that he had been able to 'start again' and that his previous history of violence could be rewritten in the light of his experience at the project.

Mention has already been made of the central role of the co-ordinator in the befriending project. In many situations she retained contact with the young person when a befriender had moved on by offering support between matches. Thus some young people viewed the co-ordinator as a mediator in difficult situations and consequently the constant figure throughout their experience of the project.

In the following example, Scott described the long-term nature of the relationship as providing a backdrop against which he could try new experiences. Scott was looked after by his mother who he recognised had 'a lot to put up with' over the years since he had been diagnosed with a medical condition. He believed that his long-term mentoring relationship with Bill had helped her to cope better with him as he had become more confident in dealing with his own life:

> *... because I have got a good friendship with Bill ken and I have had a lot of support and that because I have been working with him it will be three and a half years now ken and he ... it's basically I have always been with Bill ken, like so because I started off working with him and then it was into* [the education project] *and like Susie and that but I was still with Bill and then I was with Bill at the college and that, he used to pick me up the first few weeks and then I got into a routine of going myself and then it started gradually going down ...*
> (Education)

Key points

- Mentoring was significant for a number of participants from all three projects. They placed a high value on the opportunity to develop a trusting relationship with an unrelated adult. Qualities of trust, control, reciprocity and shared experience were valued. Someone who had experienced family problems, difficulties at school or in care, or criminal activity and who was prepared to share this, often became a key figure, providing support and advice and exploring relevant issues. The friendly nature of the relationship and the 'ability to have a laugh' with a mentor distinguished these relationships from other kinds of relationship. All of this contributed to mentoring as a safe means of reviewing areas that were risky to discuss elsewhere.

- For some participants, mentoring relationships provided a space in which to tell their story and to rehearse what they would like to do with their lives. For many it helped them to develop strategies for dealing with difficult situations and to survive in hostile environments.

- The development of a meaningful relationship was often problematic. For some young people a relationship with a befriender or a key worker was simply one of many relationships that did not include a mentoring element.

- Where mentoring was successful, the relationship had developed over time and was flexible enough to allow different approaches to be taken by both partners.

- Within the housing and education projects, contextualised knowledge and local background enabled mentors to be aware of what was going on outwith the project.

- Within the befriending project, the decontextualised nature of the relationship enabled young people to have respite from their problems but the presence of a co-ordinator acted as a link with families.

How do such relationships develop and what are the underlying processes at work?

Important changes took place in the lives of many participants between the two rounds of interviews: within the housing and education projects, a number of young people had left completely or had moved on to another part of the overall project. Several befrienders and young people had also left, with half of the original pairings remaining matched. In the second round, it was clear that many from the housing and education projects continued to have problems and to 'get into bother'. Such 'bother' took a range of forms, from homelessness, imprisonment, relationships, serious drug misuse and alcohol problems, to health issues, including sexual problems, dealing with violence and anger and so on.

Within such a context, the establishment of mentoring relationships was not always straightforward. It took time and considerable effort by both partners, and progress was often uneven. Some young people valued the processes of developing the relationship as much if not more than the outcomes. It was evident too that many relationships were fragile and easily undermined: in some cases the relationships remained marginal to the rest of their lives. In this example, Colin dismissed the time spent with one key worker during his suspension from school, as merely instrumental:

> Yes I played pool with him but I still didn't like him. But I put up with him. It was either that or … basically nothing. It passed the day when everyone else was at school.
> (Education)

Colin contrasted this with a more meaningful relationship with his first key worker who became a confidante and advised on relationships, work, health and personal anxieties:

> Well I know I can trust her … I can talk to her but I know that I can't if you know what I am getting at. She always told me that if it was something really serious she would have to mention it…
> (Education)

Some young people described how difficult they found it to open up and feel comfortable about discussing these personal issues:

> Natalie: Yes, most of the problems I have got, is about myself, about things that make me greet [cry] and everything and I dinna like to greet in front of everybody so it is only like Susie and that that has seen me cry like at [the education project]…

> Researcher: What is it about her?

> Natalie: I think it is just that she is bubbly and [laughs] she is sensible and she is stupid. [affectionately]

> Researcher: [Laughs] It's cos she is a cookery teacher, isn't it?

> Natalie: [Low and laughs] and she canna cook!
> (Education Project)

In a later interview the mentor (Susie), described her interaction with Natalie as based on agreements that they would learn together – a recognition that she could learn from the young people. She believed that very few joined the project with any belief that they had something to offer and that her task was to change this. Her lack of cooking skills was a running joke with project staff and young people. Cookery sessions were an opportunity to sit around the table to chat, discuss what was going on away from the main group setting and to engage in a practical activity that allowed the young people to 'fiddle' with their hands and get involved at a level they felt was 'safe'. Thus cooking skills were secondary to establishing a comfortable climate for the group. This mentor was often approached by young people outside the project since she lived locally and walked her dog in a local park at times when young people were around. Often more delicate issues were raised in this setting. For a number of young women and young men, this out-of-hours accessibility reinforced feelings of reciprocity and of the relationship as special.

Significant relationships

Young people described how some relationships progressed through stages to become a mutually supportive one. In this example, Rory reported on how the conversations with his befriender changed:

> … I mean we used to just sit there and talk about who his last youth group person was, gradually we just talk about whatever, you know, what the issues

are, and recently he came round to play games at my house and it was just like having one of my friends round.
(Befriending)

For others, the discovery that they could confide in an adult made the relationship meaningful and moved it on:

Yeah you could speak to her about things more than your mum, some things you could speak more about, some things you can't speak to your mum about.
(Befriending)

Some claimed to know instantly that they would get on with their befriender or key worker, jumping several stages. Lorna (Profile 3) gives a typical example of how she felt intuitively that it was safe to trust Brenda:

Yeah, we did, I remember the first time I saw her and I was like that [looks shocked]. It was just her appearance, and I was like, ohhh, but I knew straightaway that I would get on with her, and I did, she was just like, honest and friendly and that.
(Befriending)

For others it was more difficult to put this into words as Colin described one of his mentors as the exception to his rule of 'I don't trust adults you see':

I like Susie though. I don't know what it is. She is different. I don't know what it is.
(Education)

He had gradually got to know Susie over several months, choosing to join her cookery group and then seeking her out on an individual basis. His previous bad experiences of disclosing sensitive information had made him very cautious and he clearly 'tested out' how Susie reacted at each stage, before trusting her.

Negotiation

Building young people's skills in negotiation was an early goal for all the projects. For befrienders

much of this took place in relation to activities. It was clear from the accounts given by young people that such negotiation was often a novel experience and one they valued as setting the friendly tone of the relationship. Within the education and housing projects, negotiation took place over individual education plans, outdoor activities, running a flat, but also appropriate behaviour. However most of this centred on boundary setting for interaction and both workers and young people recounted anecdotes about tussles over reaching a shared understanding and agreement. Thus Colin talked about how his key worker made him get out of his car and walk home when they had an argument. Colin viewed this as a turning point in the relationship, and one which both partners treated with humour when he returned to the project.

Scott had moved on but continued to see Bill, his mentor, on an occasional basis. He carefully pointed out that this was negotiated in advance:

I just phone, well the days that I am in I just say I will be coming in to speak to you and we will sit down and we will speak. I speak about things … it hasn't changed I see him less that's all … he's just been there as a friend as well ken.
(Education)

Scott reflected that he had come to terms with many of his problems and attributed this to age and his ability to manage his medical condition. To a lesser extent he felt that the project staff group had helped him in dealing with relationships with others in a more constructive way:

Like they were ken helping me control myself, like control myself in like a bad situation and ken it was like is it worth having an argument over something small and like losing your head over something that it is not worth losing it over. And they have given me a lot of support and that because they got me back into school and that part time and I got my chance to sit my exams and that and got me into college and all that.
(Education)

He contrasted this with the situation at college where he believed the different climate left him feeling powerless to deal with staff. In this situation he was unable to put into practice the skills that he had learned and gave up his course:

Well I was meant to get help with my theory and that and all these meetings were meant to get arranged but it never happened, I never got told about them so ... and they never happened so ... ken they should have happened before I started the college, saying like it you need help then we ... will put you in like ... not put you into another class but ken if you need help then we are here ken, and I never got told any of that, it was just a basic like you go into college ken, you do this you do that and then after I left ken everyone was saying all these meetings were getting set up but I never heard about them so ...
(Education)

Even where mentoring was regarded as significant, a move to other settings often led to reduced contact as the young person balanced his/her priorities. In the education and housing projects, a move often led to the substitution of the key worker with another or with the ending of the relationship by the agency. It was here that negotiation was less evident, with contact reducing often with tacit consent by both parties. Within the befriending project, contact sometimes tailed off with fewer meetings arranged and longer intervals in between, as Rory suggests:

Researcher: Ah, right, so that has kind of tailed off recently?

Rory: That is because of my job, we used to meet on Saturday afternoons and now I am working. But after this job, I am really doing it for work experience and I really want to get something else with better hours and I will be able to start going out with Stewart again.
(Befriending)

Disclosure, trust and confidentiality

For many, the opportunity to negotiate with a mentor was a novel experience and one which brought risks as well as benefits. Some young people described a subtle process of negotiation whereby the young person disclosed sensitive information to the mentor, knowing it would be shared with other staff. Others viewed staff disclosures in certain situations as part of the deal that was agreed with the mentor at the outset of the relationship and would tailor their disclosures accordingly.

In some instances, young people viewed professionals' and key workers' sharing of information about them as undermining the mentoring element but others accepted this as part of the process. For one young woman, discussion about this issue was the catalyst to a more meaningful relationship:

I did feel let down by her once like I didn't know she had to tell stuff to my social worker and I told her stuff that was confidential and I didn't want anyone to know and my social worker found out and that ... but it was ok in the end because she explained what the routine was and that and like she apologised and everything and it was like she didn't mean it. And like she has not done it again since that and I would tell her things that are really important.
(Education)

Many believed that some discretion could be exercised about disclosure, and that the young person should be able to negotiate this to some extent with the mentor. Still others viewed disclosure to parents or other professionals as a betrayal of trust and likely to deter them from trusting the worker in future. For these individuals, it was the potential to share private information in the knowledge that it would go no further that distinguished mentoring from other relationships.

Some claimed to have confronted workers who had betrayed their trust and to have gained assurances that they would not do this in the future. Young people were often strategic about what information to share, when to share it and what not to share. Many in the befriending project felt that they had little 'risky' information to withhold.

The relationship between trust and confidentiality was a complex area loaded with different interpretations and meanings for all participants. All were aware of project guidelines on confidentiality. However these were often viewed as open for negotiation with individual mentors. Most young people were adamant that the respecting of confidential information by the mentor was essential for a trusting relationship. This was where mismatches between mentors' accounts and young people's accounts were most evident, with mentors likely to claim they adhered to the rules, and young people interpreting 'good' mentoring as about being flexible over these.

For Teresa (Profile 1), the lack of privacy in the housing project had come as a shock to her, and she felt that this had not been negotiated in any way. She felt that the staff group had gathered information about her life without her involvement:

Researcher: Have you had a key worker before this?

T: No.

Researcher: So what is that like?

T: Well it is … just, weird like. Cos in here everybody knows everything about you. Like your past, well not so much your past but mostly things that have happened recently and that and that is scary as they know things about you that you are not meant to know or something …
(Housing)

Although some young people felt this openness was an advantage, in allowing them to confront their problems, others were critical about their lack of control over who had information about their lives. Staff were clear that they did not share information with other young people, but the general air of the house was one of discussion between young people about what had happened the previous evening, health issues, forthcoming court cases, likely sentences and previous behaviour. It was also the case that very intense but often short-lived relationships developed between tenants in the project and that sensitive information sometimes became a powerful currency between young people in the group.

A shift from a laissez-faire approach to a more rule-bound environment in the wake of the eviction of the first cohort of tenants led one participant to say that he had been let down by not being able to negotiate the nature of support. He felt that the house had become an extension of a children's home with information being held by staff and that he had little opportunity to negotiate this.

Endings and timing

Timing played an important part in the mentoring relationships. Some dilemmas around negotiation became apparent in the discussions about timing and endings. By the second round of interviews, many of the relationships had changed, some had ended and in some, the level of intensity had shifted.

Some participants felt that badly managed endings or the sense of loss they had experienced, undermined previously reported benefits, as Sara suggested in Profile 2. Within the education project, some young people expressed a view that they had been abandoned by the project in the second round of interviews. Others agreed with workers that the tapering off of contact pointed up their success in becoming independent. Short-term continuations, which included transport to college, informal support and sessions with a key worker, were eagerly taken up and sometimes bridged the gap successfully. Such outreach demanded sensitive handling to ensure that young people were not stigmatised by the presence of key workers or did not become more, rather than less, dependent on the key worker.

Balancing this was difficult and a number had left college and dropped contact with the project. Little evidence existed to suggest that the further education colleges viewed themselves as having any role in supporting such vulnerable young people.

Some young people expressed anger and disappointment when their befriender moved on. Others were more philosophical, seeing this as inevitable. Some had actively chosen to leave the relationship and viewed this as 'growing out' of the need for a befriender. Eric, for example felt that he had outgrown his mentor's image of him. They had met for three years and Eric now felt that his mentor could not offer the more reciprocal relationship he sought:

> I was starting to get more confident and feeling more like that I was you know that I could be just friends with the people that were taking me out instead of them being the person that was looking after me, them being the adult and me being the kid basically, I felt like it was moving a bit away from that and more towards, by that time I was about 13 or 14, and more towards, mm, us just being friends sort of thing.
> (Befriending)

One young woman had developed a strong relationship with her befriender and neglected her own network of friends. In the first round of interviews Lesley was attending college and identified a number of key people in her social network; by the second round of interviews, she had left college, disregarded people who she had previously seen as sources of support and become extremely isolated. Throughout this period her befriender was one of the few people with whom Lesley maintained contact. On the one hand this relationship had sustained Lesley through a very difficult time and had offered a constant source of

support and advice. On the other, over-reliance on it may have led her to focus on this relationship rather than get to know others. In this sense, one-to-one mentoring could inhibit as well as encourage the development of 'natural' social relationships.

Many young people noted a lasting effect and a continuing affection for their mentor, even where the relationship had formally ended. Some relationships lasted well beyond the intervention. For some the interaction shifted into another gear, as with Teresa and Duncan who maintained contact by telephone.

Clearly, some mentoring relationships required a timescale that was relatively open ended. When this process was disrupted, the potential benefits were easily dissipated, as the following quotation suggests:

> I got on with her really good. I was doing that book, you know the Azdan book – like you do different activities in it and that and then at the end of it you get like a certificate just to say you have achieved it and that. But I had done half the book and then they kept like changing support workers so really I lost doing the book, I never ever finished it but I would like to go back and finish it.
> (Education)

Maria reflected that for her, the timing of the intervention had been inappropriate. She had walked out of the project:

> … well they tried to help me as much as they could but I wouldn't let them. Cos I just tried to do things myself – oh sure I would let them help me with some things but ken I just tried to do everything by my own accord. So it is not that I am saying that it is not my fault … or anybody else – I don't think it was anyone's help I think it was just my attitude.
> (Education)

After dropping contact with the project, she had been thrown out by her parents, began using a range of substances and got involved in a number of illegal activities. Reflecting on this, she claimed it was largely a fear of going to prison that motivated her to change this pattern, rather than any support she was offered either by her family or by key workers:

> I'm not sure ... well I have grown up and I've wisened up as well. Cos I can't be bothered getting into trouble and that. It's not as if I need it nowadays, ken, I have been threatened with jail and ken I dinna want to go to jail. And if I stick with this probation, there is nothing else [no more charges] to go up for. So that is all right ...
> (Education)

In one respect, it was when she was trying to reinvent herself as a 'normal' and law abiding young person that mentoring support had been helpful. In telling the story of her difficulties she reflected that she was now in a better position to understand her problems and those of others, such as her younger brother who had begun to follow her earlier lead. She expressed some regret for rejecting the support and felt that she would make better use of the mentoring in her current situation:

> I did really enjoy going there. And I wish I never left but like I mean you stop going to it anyway [when you are 16] but I wish I had still stayed with my workers and that just ... because for a while after it I just went all to pot and I just never did nothing.
> (Education)

Relationships with key workers in the housing project were often complicated by the latter's managerial responsibilities. A court case with tenants who had trashed their flats reinforced this tension, with several of the original intake of young people being sent to prison and staff being cited as witnesses in court. As a result, all contact ended between these young people and the project. This raises questions about how mentoring support can be sustained with those young people who go

beyond the boundaries. One ex-resident commented:

> Well I know I let them down, but I felt let down by them.
> (Housing)

Although he no longer had formal contact with the project, he phoned his former key worker on a regular basis, invited him to his wedding, and on leaving prison, looked to him for advice and challenge:

> I've always got on well with him. He helped me through a lot at the house ... he knew how to speak to me and that ... he could just explain things from another point of view and that ... I don't know I just took a shine to him. I would listen to him and I never used to listen to anybody else. I would listen to him and he would point me in the right direction and that ... he was like one of the boys really, like he knew how to have a good laugh and that ...
> (Housing)

David, who was also evicted from the housing project, told a similar story at his second interview. On joining the project he had expected to live independently and to negotiate any support he needed. However, he soon viewed the staff as controlling and complained that they did not respect his desire for privacy. The exception was a worker who had left during his tenancy whom he described as 'younger and more like me'. David claimed that he had been 'the blue-eyed boy' with staff at the beginning but that this had changed when he had challenged their control. At the first interview he had been more positive about the project, reporting that he would seek support from staff. Later he claimed that he would only seek support from his girlfriend who was also an ex-tenant, but felt that he was otherwise isolated. Since going to prison he had no formal contact with the project, had no contact with his family and very occasional contact with his previous foster parents.

His only contact with services was with the agency who checked on his electronic tag. He reflected that the mentoring on offer had not 'been for me' although he recognised that it suited his girlfriend. The claim that staff attempted to control young people was not repeated by others in the housing or education projects. Nevertheless this example highlights the delicate balance between interference and support for young people who may regard too much of their lives as being public knowledge.

Uncertainty over timescales led many in this sample to be strategic about the level of commitment they were prepared to invest in such relationships, fearing that they might be hurt if the relationship became too important. This was often mentioned in relation to negative previous experiences with people in their lives. Less frequently mentioned was an inconsistency by workers. However Jane was the exception here:

Just like, I had been looking forward to going out and then I just couldn't really be bothered with her any more, because she just cancelled it five times.
(Befriending)

A number of young people faced the ending of relationships when they 'moved on', whether this was to prison or to more positive situations. For some this loss of a source of support came at a time when they were extremely vulnerable. This was well understood by project staff in all projects and was a recurring subject of discussion throughout the life of the study. Within the befriending project this was less problematic since the emphasis was more heavily on building a relationship outwith the usual social context of the young person.

Points of transition seemed to be a testing time for relationships with key workers. Sara explained that when she had to adjust to a new situation, she was not prepared for the abrupt ending of her relationship with her key worker:

I still feel that he dropped me, they just dropped me as soon as I went into college, and that was it, once

she is in college she will be fine. I was really close to him and I trusted him and everything. I used to talk to him about things but it has just changed.
(Education)

She felt that she had lost control over the relationship and that she could no longer negotiate with the project staff. Her earlier assumption that the relationship went beyond professional boundaries was challenged and left her feeling that she had been rejected by the mentor. Later in the interview, she described how she had negotiated help within the college. This suggested that she was now more able to seek support from other sources:

I have gone to study support at the college and they are helping me out with my theory homework and stuff so we are all getting on top of it.
(Education)

Although she agreed that she was more confident since going to college, when the interviewer asked if lessons from her relationship with her key worker at the education project had helped her in securing this help she was indignant:

No, no it didn't help at all ... did not help me one bit. It just sustained me.
(Education)

However although face-to-face contact with Pilar, a worker in another project, had decreased, the bond remained and provided a useful backdrop to new experiences as Sara indicated:

[I sometimes] see them, not all the time ... before I came here to meet you I nipped in to see Pilar, I was really close to her, I liked her. I still am [close] ... a wee bit.
(Education)

She had also developed a close relationship with her foster carer:

I have a right good chat with her and she speaks my language ken, we are just close and I will tell her

about anything really, I will just be upfront and she is
upfront with me if I am like …
(Education)

Later, she contradicted her earlier statement about the relationship with her key worker/mentor when she reflected that he had helped her to approach new relationships in a different way. This suggests that her experiences of a group of mentors had helped her to forge new relationships and may have contributed to her new confidence in her own abilities.

In other instances the continuation of mentoring was casual: Natalie lived near one key worker from the education project who often gave her a lift into town if he was passing by. During this they would chat and catch up on news. Another woman worker at the education project was known to walk her dog in the park, a favourite spot for hanging out and one where young people often felt able to approach her for advice, to crack a joke or to catch up on gossip. Others negotiated dropping in for a chat with workers on an occasional basis. In this respect the mentoring played some part in reinforcing a sense of community and belonging within neighbourhoods where such young people were otherwise regarded with suspicion.

Within the housing project, phone calls to particular workers were a frequently used means of contact after moving out. A few young people phoned workers at home and visited on occasions. This contact was highly valued by those young people who had moved on and who were struggling to establish a new friendship group or to reinvent themselves away from the friends with whom they 'got into trouble'. Workers themselves were often more ambivalent about how these were negotiated and managed.

A move to new accommodation usually signalled a change in key worker support and the ending of a mentoring relationship. Not only was this a change of worker but a change of team. A

number of young people in the study expressed criticism of their new key worker, often complaining that they adopted a more managerial role than the housing project staff.

When David was in jail, having 'fallen out' with the project, his mentor was one of the few people to visit and, importantly to the young man, he did this in his own time. He continued to phone him, 'not for advice just for a chat as I rely on my girlfriend to help me with problems now'. However he continued to meet his mentor for social events and valued the relationship.

Lorna was aware from the outset that her befriender planned an extensive trip abroad. Nevertheless she was still upset and found it difficult to accept this as an ending and expressed a hope that the relationship would resume on Brenda's return:

L: Yeah, I always knew it was going to happen,
because she says it practically from the start.

Researcher: So did that make it easier, or …

L: Harder I would say.

Researcher: Yeah, in what way?

L: Sort of, I don't know, I know, the fact that I knew
that she was leaving, and would go, you know, I am
leaving, and I would go, ohhh, I know, and it just
made it even worse knowing that she would leave,
do you know what I mean.

When a befriender ended the relationship, dealing with the loss was difficult and was often interpreted as rejection. For Amanda, Susan's departure had been distressing and had led her to re-evaluate the importance of the relationship:

They were just people that I have lost, Susan, I wrote
to her, but then she just disappeared. I hate people
who just disappear, it is like anything in life, you put
so much effort in to it, and it is like why the fuck do
you put so much effort in to it and like they disappear.

It is like all that effort that you put into life and it is like sometimes you don't get that much of it back. It is so stupid.
(Befriending)

Later in the interview she described how:

She left, just didn't keep in contact like she said. I hate when people say things they don't mean. And my mum is like, oh everybody says things that they don't mean. And I am like, well, when are they going to stop, eh? Aww lots of people have let me down ...

During this second interview, Amanda avoided talking about things which upset her or which she described as negative. She was awaiting a new match with a befriender from an adult befriending project but expressed uncertainty as to whether she wished to pursue this after her previous experience. Despite this she participated eagerly in both rounds of interviews for the study.

Eric, who had a succession of befrienders over the ten years that he was involved in the project, was more philosophical:

I felt like it was a shame as I had got to know him really well, and you know I had got to like him a lot as a good friend, because he was someone that I had got on really well with, so I felt it was like, it was a shame, because I felt like I was losing a friend when he moved on.
(Befriending)

Treats for bad boys and girls

A complaint from some professional staff outside the housing and education projects was that the projects rewarded bad behaviour by providing treats and paying attention to small groups of difficult young people. Staff in both projects were well aware of this criticism and pointed to the complex and multiple needs of the target group.

It was clear that the majority of users of the education project valued the support it provided.

Partly this was about having some control over the educational process, for others it was about the relaxed climate, but for many it was about the chance to learn at their own pace:

When I was coming here part time I really enjoyed it. But when they put me here full time I've been better off. It's better off here than other schools because you can talk more clearly about things – it's one-to-one work and they have got time for you, they don't force you to do anything that you don't want to do ... you get to choose your timetable instead of just being given it.
(Education)

Within the befriending project young people were more likely to be constructed as 'deserving' and as missing out in some way through no 'fault' of their own. Other professionals viewed them as deserving of opportunities that other children received as a matter of course. A social worker indicated that she frequently referred siblings of children who were having problems to the befriending project as she felt this could offer some treats. This influenced the initial views of some young people about the purposes of befriending:

Lorna: No, see at the start I thought, oh, it is just free places, to go places for free, but see, it must have been the second week and I thought, it was just a really good relationship, well, friendship should I say, and it was just brilliant, it really was.
(Befriending)

A befriender expressed discomfort with how one young person interpreted the intervention as a source of free services:

I quite liked him but I think he felt that he was just there for the outings and I was thinking, money, money rather than [that we were] going out and enjoying himself.
(Befriending)

Within the education project, concern to build up a relationship often meant working on joint activities which might not otherwise have been within the reach of the young person or their family. Similarly the activities supported by the housing project were offered as part of a package. This entailed working alongside the key worker to resolve difficulties or develop strategies to tackle deep-seated issues.

A consensus existed about the importance of creating a safe space in which young people could rehearse their versions of events, of who they wanted to be and reflect on the ways in which they felt that they had 'messed up' or that others had 'messed them about'. By the second round, this was often reported as if it was something which was no longer on offer. Some young people had developed caring relationships with others but some felt isolated and uncertain about their capacity to sustain these. Importantly a number had developed a repertoire of skills which they could then use to develop their own relationships and to offer support to others.

Key points

- The processes of building up and sustaining mentoring relationships could be problematic but often offered an opportunity to test out ideas and identities.

- Issues of trust and confidentiality were complex and subject to negotiation.

- Balancing dependence and autonomy required considerable work by mentors and young people.

- Continuity was important and management of this demanded careful planning.

- Endings had the potential to undermine the immediate benefits perceived by young people and to reinforce feelings of rejection.

- The opportunity to sustain an informal relationship on an occasional basis beyond the intervention was of value – keeping this door open could be an important link for young people who are excluded from other kinds of provision or who fail on leaving the project.

- Other agencies did not always share similar approaches to work with vulnerable young people.

How do young people interpret planned mentoring relationships, as opposed to informal relationships, within their existing social networks?

In this section we examine findings about relationships described as meaningful, including those within families. We explore issues arising about the role of family, gender and friendship, themes that have often been overlooked in discussions of planned mentoring. We then consider how relationships with particular professionals or befrienders are understood and explore barriers to the development of mentoring relationships.

Family relationships

With few exceptions, young people identified their mothers as the most important people within their social networks and as key sources of advice and support. This was the case even where family relationships were difficult, and where the young person was being cared for elsewhere. Ideas about the qualities of a 'proper mother' guided some of the descriptions and clearly influenced views about other relationships with adults. Such descriptions were often highly stereotypical and based on a very gendered vision of the family as a 'safe haven', which seemed at odds with many actual accounts of family life.

Thus in the first round of interviews, Sara – who was brought up mainly by her stepfather and in foster care – described her mother as a poor parent, commenting:

Her parental boundaries aren't good enough and she's not like suitable to look after me or [my sister].
(Education)

Although she considered her mum to 'be a bad influence' she viewed her as the person who was closest to her and to whom she could 'talk about anything'. By the second round when she was living in foster care she met with her mother regularly after several months of no contact:

Your mum is your mum. You fall out with your mum so I would cope with it better now, it's just that I couldn't cope with it at the time.
(Education)

Some young people seemed to take it for granted that their mother would be the first person to whom they would turn for support or to solve problems. However some would seek advice elsewhere and some suggested that their mother deserved shielding from particularly difficult issues such as drug use, or other illicit behaviour, as Teresa stated:

T: I can speak to my mum but I can speak to Jessie about different things that are like, more important, well not more important but …

Researcher: So what kind of things?…

T: [pause] Just like how I am feeling, and if I am upset or something because my mum usually gets upset if I am upset because she is just that kind of person.
(Housing)

Norman made a similar comment about his relationship with his father who had taken on the role of principal carer. Within the sample, only one other participant had lived with a father when the relationship between parents had broken down:

Talk to my dad about anything – but I'm worried about hurting him … we were really close and that, but we are not so close now since I have been doing drugs and that. But we can still talk about anything so [I would look for help from] *my dad or my psychologist or Maria.*
(Education)

Alongside this some young people were likely to go to some lengths to keep such relationships going, as Colin explained:

If I fall out with my mum, I just go to my room. If I fall out with anyone else World War 3 breaks out.
(Education)

By the second round Colin reported that his relationship with his mother had improved and he felt that she was beginning to trust him more after a difficult period when he was in trouble with the police. He described the relationship as more reciprocal and negotiated; a more mature relationship that gave him a lot of support.

Participants were swift to defend mothers, or to explain their actions, as in this excerpt from the first interview with Sara who explained her problems with her mother as follows:

I think it was because my mam is so young and she had me so young. She is 32 and she had me at 16 or 17 so she didn't have the time to go out and be wild and that.
(Education)

However, many family relationships were difficult and for some young people there was a constant shunting between living with different family members, being in care and sleeping on friends' floors. Thus, by the second round, Norman had spent a brief period living with his mother. He had gone to some lengths to do this, returning to make a case at the children's panel. He had fallen out with his father whom he felt was neglecting him in favour of other children. In a previous interview, Norman had referred to his mother as having serious drug problems and as violent and had explained that his key worker felt moving in with his mother was a mistake. Subsequently he dropped out of the education project, lost contact with his key worker and resumed misusing drugs. When his relationship with his mother deteriorated, he returned to his father, who later threw him out. He was now living with foster parents, visiting his father fortnightly and described himself as trying to make amends and become a better role model for his younger brother. When interviewed for this study, Norman's father was adamant that he felt unable to cope with Norman's drug use and mental health problems. Norman's actions had also, he felt, had a negative effect on his younger brother. In his opinion, Norman's decision to move in with his mother, who was addicted to heroin, had undone the benefits of the mentoring he received at the education project. His father reported that project staff had gone to great lengths to support both Norman and himself but he believed that Norman's rejection of this support left little hope for his future. In contrast, Norman reported that the mentoring had helped him to rebuild his life after this series of incidents.

This finding about young people's loyalty to parents is clearly not new and accords with findings from a number of studies. But what is important here is that mentoring provided young people with the skills to negotiate with parents, to rebuild relationships and where necessary to seek support elsewhere. Mentors themselves often adopted or were cast in quasi-parenting roles, leading some young people to describe mentors as 'my second mother'. More often, meaningful relationships with key workers were complementary to family relationships, allowing young people to reflect on and revisit family issues. The chance to discuss such issues with mentors often enabled young people to develop new

insights into family problems. In some cases, mentoring provided a template with which young people could negotiate with their families.

Parental contact with the projects varied widely. The majority of interviewees in the education project felt that their parents had been grateful for the help the project had offered. Some young people actively tried to develop links between their key workers and their parents, for example Scott encouraged his mentor to drop in for tea with his mother. Casual contact was evident between workers and parents of young people who were living at home when young people were collected to transport them to and from the project. Others were more inclined to keep family and mentoring relationships separate. Within the befriending project, befrienders were more likely to focus on the young person and usually remained distanced from other family members. Some befrienders made a point of collecting young people outside the home to reinforce this distance. Within the housing project, some parents visited, while others had little or no contact with young people and project staff. Within all three projects, some parents declined any involvement.

Peers and friends

From the ethnographic work it was clear that intense peer relationships developed between young people within the projects. For some of the young women, in particular, these provided a source of both support and tension, with a number pointing out in the second round that they spent considerable time and energy in avoiding former acquaintances. A number of those in the education project tried to build new friendship groups which led them to prefer to meet friends away from home or to start afresh in settings where their history was not known. Many of the young women in the housing and education projects pointed to close friends as important sources of support and guidance.

One young woman reflected that when she lived at the housing project she had felt at the mercy of the young men who dominated the house:

I was the only quine [girl] in the project at that time and I had no-one to hang out with except them [the other tenants]. And they were all getting into trouble and so I just did too. And if I drink, I just shout and go mad and that and it wasn't good and that is how I ended up in jail.
(Housing)

Although she was now living with one of these young men, they both tried to avoid the rest of the group. She pointed out that this was very difficult in a small community where her reputation made it difficult to make new friends. She now felt less in need of friends since her attention was focused on her baby and husband and she got support from professionals. Her efforts to be a 'good mother' had won respect from workers at the project and she hoped to continue her contact with them.

In the second round of interviews, some young people described how they drew on their own experience of mentoring in their strategies to support others, as in this example of Natalie and her cousin:

and she came to me and it just makes me feel better that she is speaking, that she feels she can trust me and that. And I would like to stay for her – it's like she was saying, 'Oh Natalie when I am starting I can come and speak to you', and I was, 'Oh but you will have Janie to speak to,' and she went, 'I just want to come and talk to you,' so I have got that.
(Education)

This was not always successful but their willingness to risk this and their confidence in offering support to others was significantly different from accounts given in the first round.

Natalie follows up the last point about her potential to mentor others by stating that, having encountered difficulties, she was in a good position to understand others:

say you were coming to me and say you came to me and you were upset and that. See if I was always a happy person, I don't think I would be able to tell you what to do because like I had never been unhappy myself. So like the things that have happened to me and like I could speak to other folk and that about the things that happen to them. Cos like my little cousin and her mum are not like arguing, but she has just turned 13 and you know what they are like. And I have been speaking to her and that and like she understands that that she canna' be like I was when I was younger. So she knows ... that she can just go so far to push it.
(Education)

In both rounds of interviews, Teresa talked about becoming a counsellor. She believed she could develop the skills that her key worker used and her own experience:

Researcher: You said earlier that you would like to be a drugs and alcohol counsellor – where has that come from?

T: I don't know but it's probably being here because there's not like, Maria she is like a counsellor, not an alcohol and drug counsellor, but that is probably why it is so easy to speak to her about your problems cos she has been through all the training and it's like ... I want to be an alcohol and drug counsellor because people in my family have had drug [problems] and a lot of my ex boyfriends have been alcoholics.

A similar point was made by a young woman in the befriending project:

Researcher: ... so do you think you could be a befriender?

L: I would like to be, yeah, I really would, I thought about it, but then I don't know, but see now when I think about it, I think I would because it is not selfish it is a two way thing. I mean I would be getting something and the child would be getting something as well, do you know what I mean. So you are helping them, but in return, you are getting something from them as well.

Researcher: Yeah, and what would you be offering them?

L: I suppose just if they had any problems, like just being there.
(Befriending)

Gender

The majority of young people said that they would see women as the most likely mentors, as John suggested:

There would be ... understanding workers in this place, mostly women I would say, if you want to talk to someone.
(Education)

Similarly, Jane was reluctant to confide in a male worker at the housing project but found it difficult to articulate why this was the case:

Well he's a man and I'm not too keen on speaking to a man as much as I am a woman. I don't know what it is. It depends on what kind of thing. Paul is pretty easy going but I don't know.
(Housing)

Young women in general felt more comfortable discussing health issues with women and this often prefaced statements that this meant they would see women as more understanding of intimate issues such as sexual relationships. Natalie reiterated a reluctance to discuss personal issues with a man although she felt comfortable with male workers:

My sister Angela, she was the person I was most able to speak to. I didna speak to my dad because he was like male and that. My sister Angela had been through it all so I could really speak to her.
(Education)

However this was not always clear cut. Scott claimed that the gender of his mentor was very important and that he would be unlikely to discuss matters with a man. But later in the interview he identified a particular male worker as the person that he would approach if his (female) key worker was unavailable. Scott claimed that he could speak to this man because they did a lot of activities together and he trusted him.

For three of the young women, cooking together with a woman worker cemented their relationship with her and enabled them to discuss issues as a group. Marianne, who left at the beginning of the study to take up a college course, was later recognised as a source of support and advice to other young women at the project by two of the interviewees. Partly this was because she was one of the few graduates of the project who had sustained her college course, and partly because she retained links with both the project and friends that she had made there. Marianne was viewed as acting as a mentor for this group by both staff and young people, for although she continued to experience difficulties, she had 'moved on' into the world of work that lay outside the project and retained her commitment to her friendship group.

Young women were more likely to emphasise the importance of someone who had experienced difficult relationships, particularly with male partners and who, they suggested, could empathise with their problems. Women who were 'mother figures' and who had brought up their own children were also seen as reliable and supportive, and often held up as ideal types of 'good mothers'. This was not exclusive, however, with others preferring to talk to workers who had similar interests and social lives. Within the befriending project, in particular, younger befrienders who could introduce new interests and who were interested in 'having fun' appealed to many of the participants and this often offset the disadvantages of a short-term relationship.

Male mentors appealed when they combined an ability to listen and to provide emotional support with interests shared by the young people. For many young men, key workers offered an acceptable male role model and a set of behaviours that they could emulate. For some young men, the combination of a 'macho' image, for example a mechanic or biker, with a caring approach was important. Some young men were adamant that they would not disclose family or emotional issues to any workers, but sometimes contradicted this with examples of talking through an issue arising within the family with a female worker.

Key points

- Family relationships, particularly relationships with mothers, were highly valued even where these were problematic. A key benefit of a good mentoring relationship was in helping young people to come to terms with parental relationships.

- Peer relationships could be both supportive and negative but there was little work done with peer groups.

- Making new friends was risky and problematic, particularly in rural areas because of the difficulties of 'living down' reputations. Some evidence showed that mentoring relationships assisted in addressing this.

- Mentoring relationships often allowed young people to explore different aspects of their identities.

- Good mentoring was often a starting point for young people to consider their own skills in supporting others.

- Mentoring was often perceived as a safe way of addressing difficulties that young people faced.

- Although mentoring was frequently perceived as a process undertaken by women, evidence existed of different forms.

- Fears about being let down made some young people uncertain of the value of the intervention and sometimes increased feelings of risk and vulnerability.

- Control over information and the sharing of information was important.

- Moving out of the projects or changing living arrangements often brought issues about the nature of mentoring relationships to light.

- Young people often reviewed the relationships more critically when they discussed endings.

- The timing of the intervention also appeared to be important, with some reflecting that they would be better able to benefit from mentoring at a later date.

6 Findings from interviews with mentors

This chapter explores the perceptions of adult mentors and analyses how these match with the accounts that have been presented in the preceding sections. A total of 15 interviews with adults took place; six were undertaken in both the education and befriending projects and three in the housing project. The sample was purposively selected to give a balance of gender and experience and to include mentors that young people had identified as 'significant' in interviews. As in the rest of the report, the term mentors is used when discussing both key workers and befrienders. We look at befrienders' and key workers' motivations for mentoring, since this will yield insights into how their understandings of their role match with those of young people. From this we go on to examine how they view their role in relation to families and other relationships. Following this we explore their views on the underlying processes, with particular attention to endings, timing and models of mentoring. In so doing we seek to highlight key issues for mentors in both paid and unpaid settings.

Motivations for mentoring

Mentors were generally motivated by a liking for young people. In all projects they reiterated the importance of empathy and a willingness to work *with* rather than *on* young people. They also expressed a desire to help those who were 'losing out' in some way. Many of those interviewed expressed the opinion that many young people were ill equipped to deal with the situations in which they found themselves.

Alongside this many believed that the young people that they worked with were in need of some kind of support outside the family. Within the befriending project, respite and 'time out' from difficult circumstances were frequently mentioned. Within the education and housing projects, key workers more often emphasised their role as one of

bringing out latent skills and supporting behavioural change. Mentoring also offered some potential for workers to develop a new career and to build on skills gained in the community or in bringing up children. Thus some befrienders volunteered in order to gain experience before committing to training or paid work. Some key workers had progressed from voluntary youth work to part-time paid work as temporary or relief workers and had thus become semi-professional workers almost by accident. Some mentors from all projects were fully trained professionals in social work, youth work or teaching who were attracted by the notion of working with young people outside formal settings.

The mentor's role in relation to families and other relationships

Family and risky pasts

A number of key workers referred to their own backgrounds as a springboard to work with young people. In the education project, for example, Susie reflected that her own history of 'being a bit of a tearaway' helped her to make connections with young people. Another was motivated by a conviction that strong family relationships had helped her to avoid difficulties that faced many of the young people that she worked with:

> we've got kids that are pushing the boundaries that wee bit and that wee bit, where I had my mother and father saying, 'No that's not what you do and this is the consequences of that', the majority of these kids don't have that.
> (Education)

Annie believed that her own experience of a disrupted home life provided her with important insights into the needs of vulnerable young people. She believed someone brought up in a more conventional way might have difficulty in recognising the issues:

Yeah, I think it is maybe more important having someone who has done that and not a ... a horrible home life but not a good one you know like my parents split up and everything. [Lowers voice] Like you will get a social worker who has come from nothing but a good environment and they will come out with something and I just wouldn't do it like that, or say that ...
(Housing)

But although experience with bringing up children was useful, it was not a straightforward transfer:

You are building up with your own child because you are with them all the time ... you are building up that kind of relationship ... with children that you haven't grown up with, it is trying to find what works with them if you know what I mean.
(Befriending)

Most key workers and befrienders, even those with a 'tearaway' past, viewed their current, more ordered reality as very different. Some felt that they acted as role models and demonstrators that it was possible to move out of a difficult life into a more normalised existence. Mentors rarely identified structural and economic constraints as barriers to the progress of young people, preferring to focus on poor family relationships and the poor socialisation of young people into appropriate behaviour.

In the following example, the befriender reflected on his own experience of adult friends outwith the family and used this as a template in mentoring:

Well, I know from my own experience how important the friendship of somebody other than my parents was to me. In fact, I can think of two older men, who were very, very important to me when I was an adolescent and beyond. So I kind of have this, I suppose, personal feeling that that kind of thing can be very valuable to any young person. You know

parents are important but I think somebody outside the family can also be very important and I think I feel very lucky in the contact that I had with these two men.
(Education)

For others, offering a safe space in which young people could build up their confidence and gain reassurance was a key element, as for this key worker who shared her own experiences with the young person:

Well I mean, confidence, gives them security, they don't feel as though they are different from anybody else, I don't think, well myself, I try and make them feel normal and they will come out with things like oh this happened and that happened and I will say well this happened to me, this is what happened to me. And it's I've done this and I've done that and it gives them a sense that they are not on their own. Other people have been through what they have been through, and it makes them feel a bit better because they know other people have been through it. And that they are not on their own, that they have people that care about them and who want them in here and want to be in their company. And they get encouraged to do things.
(Housing)

Allied to this was a perception that many vulnerable young people demonstrated a high degree of resilience. Within both the education and housing projects, mentors believed that some young people had dealt with some extreme situations and that judgements about their current behaviour had to be viewed within this context. For one male worker, it was important to work from the assumption that young people possessed resilient qualities:

And I think that some of these kids have got a lot of courage and there's a lot more to them than they often give you reason to believe.
(Education)

Individual support from an influential adult could help in bringing resilience to the surface but it was important to be realistic:

The causes are deep rooted and to iron these out takes time and some of the scars are there and they'll never disappear, they'll always be there. And they'll always affect that person as an individual and it'll either make them fight like hell or various degrees downwards you know ... I think a lot does depend on who these young people can latch onto and to whether they get a leg up as you call it or get smacked down.
(Education)

Another key worker reflected that there were very few ways in which success in dealing with difficult circumstances were recognised:

She has had to deal with a lot of rejection and of being treated badly in her relationships. She has done really well to survive it and to come out of it at all. It is never going to be easy for her.
(Housing)

Establishing relationships with family networks was viewed with some ambivalence by key workers. Such work was negotiated with the young person and was the exception rather than the rule. In many cases families were reluctant to be drawn in, some having given up on the young person. Thus key workers were more likely to focus on helping young people to develop strategies for dealing with difficult family relationships than working with families directly. However, one parent reported that the informal support the project had offered her had been invaluable and she had been dismayed when this was ended once her son moved on from the project.

Befrienders felt clearly that their prime responsibility was to 'be there' for the young person and many felt uncomfortable if they were 'drawn in' to engage with families. Given the limits of time and resources it is difficult to see how

volunteer befrienders could be expected to develop this aspect of mentoring. However, the importance that young people placed on family relationships suggests a need to engage with some of these issues.

Social networks

Both befrienders and key workers expressed a view that peer groups were likely to be negative influences on their charges. Strategies were frequently developed at an organisational level to deal with this issue. Thus within the education project, astute timetabling ensured that particular young people were unlikely to be in the building at the same time. Within the housing project, allocations were used to try to ensure a balance of tenants and to minimise the influence of 'power blocs' of young people in the aftermath of early problems with a particularly difficult group.

When group work took place within the befriending project, it was with a small number often comprising those who were awaiting matching with a befriender. Few befrienders were in contact with young people's social networks. One related an incident where this had been very uncomfortable: when and she and the befriendee had met up at a skating rink with what she viewed as an undesirable group of young people. She encountered difficulties in working with the young person as part of a group and subsequently tried to avoid this. Several befrienders had specifically chosen befriending in preference to other forms of youth work because they preferred to work on a one-to-one basis rather than with a group.

Building capacity among young people to draw on support from their social networks also evoked tensions for key workers. Clearly, helping young people to reintegrate into mainstream living is difficult where most peer relationships lie within a group known to be experiencing difficulties. At the same time, moving on may involve cutting down on support from project workers, leaving the young person isolated both from existing networks and without a safety net with which to 'risk' making new relationships.

Professional relationships

The opportunity to develop relationships free from formal constraints held appeal for many befrienders and key workers. One mentor contrasted her role with that of social workers:

... I think it is hard for them because I can give and take and I can say well, maybe you have made a mistake and whatever but I'm not in their face in the way that the social worker would have to be. So it is a different relationship.
(Education)

For another worker, the frameworks were completely at odds with each other:

We've got the luxury of spending more time with the young folk, we're able to build relationships better, maybe not better but different types of relationships because we've got the time, we've got the resources, we can take however long it takes to do a piece of work whereas a social worker might have a fortnight to get a report done. I don't know they've got so many people on their books that they can't possibly spend the time that we do.
(Housing)

To some extent these differences are illustrated by the experience of a befriender who had joined the project in order to continue a relationship with a young person for whom he had previously been a social worker. Becoming a befriender had given him flexibility to advocate for the young person, with the added advantage of using his knowledge and social work skills to challenge what he considered to be unjust decisions.

Some tensions were evident about whether the mentoring relationship was a professional relationship or a more fluid one that crossed professional boundaries. For some key workers, creating dependency was an initial aim of the work:

[She] was completely and utterly dependent on me and that was what we wanted to be honest. That's what we wanted to happen and it was okay to happen because she had so many broken attachments in her life that to build a relationship and to have an attachment with a positive adult was what we were trying to establish and it became difficult when we tried to move that on. But it took a long, long time, it took years. It took two or three years to actually get that young person to a stage where she was able to do the same type of work with someone else.

Key workers often linked this to bringing out latent skills, 'normalising' the behaviour of young people or attempting to undo the negative impact of bad experiences. Befrienders frequently expressed more limited aims: building confidence, providing time out for young people who were coping with chaotic or distressing home circumstances and being a consistent presence in an otherwise unpredictable social world. For this befriender it was important to be clear about the limits of her role:

We are not an authority figure, we are not police, we are not education, we are not social work, we are purely there to give them a wee bit of fun and to take them out of the home situation for a wee while. Whereas quite often you find that if there is a situation going on at home, grannies and aunties are quite often caught up in it anyway ...
(Befriending)

In this respect, befrienders offered a different kind of support, with less direct involvement in the social networks or family groups of the young person.

'Building up' a relationship

Both befrienders and key workers echoed young people in emphasising the importance of a voluntary relationship underpinned by co-operation and negotiation between the partners. This was often a new experience for young people who were often referred because of difficulties with social relationships. All mentors were sensitive to the importance of negotiation and the time necessary to build up trust. The mentor often had to be creative in approaching this and had to perform a delicate balancing act, particularly in the early stages:

> I think it probably does because to begin with they have the power whether or not they're going to want to meet you for a start. Ours is all voluntary, there's nobody forced to come here so they've got that initial power of, 'Yeah okay I'll buy into this'. So as far as that's concerned they have that bit of power. It does shift I think. But I think it shifts back and fore with you giving them a wee bit of responsibility and maybe they'll chuck it back in your face but you've got to try and encourage them to become independent if you like.
> (Education)

The process of building up a relationship with a young person was a vital step in the development of mentoring. Most befrienders viewed their role as mainly about the provision of shared leisure activity with any additional element an optional extra. Both befrienders and mentors expressed the view that the young person's own preferences should determine the development of the relationship. This could be an uneven process and highly demanding of mentors. One befriender felt that she was constantly being tested out by the young person. Having to call in help to get her recalcitrant charge out of a swimming pool was the final straw that led her to terminate the relationship. She felt that at every outing such 'testing out' became more, rather than less,

confrontational and that it was not moving beyond a one-sided relationship. Another befriender identified a shift as the relationship developed:

> It definitely is a two-sided thing. I suppose at the start you kind of just say it is being you that kind of puts it all in but they definitely give it back.
> (Befriending)

In situations where a young person had decided to trust the key worker, the early stages were less problematic. Many participants expressed surprise about how open young people were with adults who were previously unknown to them. One key worker believed that this demonstrated an absence of adults who could be trusted with sensitive disclosures within families:

> … she was quite open and willing to … desperate for someone to speak to I think and confide in … I think she saw it as a mutual trust and respect and she confided quite a bit so she obviously felt that she could trust me in what she was saying and I gained her respect. And I think it was just very open, I mean from day one I told her that anything that she said to me could not always be kept in confidence, you know sometimes it would have to be passed on so in that respect she knew where she stood.
> (Education)

For many befrienders the open-ended nature of the intervention held great appeal. In this example, encouraging the young person to negotiate was seen as the first stage in developing the relationship:

> … we did everything from like horse-riding to going for a picnic, to the cinema, ice-skating, bowling, it was just usually I left it up to them because they were obviously 'No, you decide' and I was like 'No, it is not … you are not going out for me, we are going out for you', you know. We went to the museum, the science place and …
> (Befriending)

Another befriender suggested that the intervention might offer a bridge to new opportunities for the young person by encouraging latent skills:

I think what I hoped that I would do would just be to not really change them at all as people because that is not what I wanted to go out and do but I suppose just to give them the opportunity to see different things and see kind of like a different part of how life can actually be. You kind of want to give them because alright some young people they especially from talking to P he just kind of thought 'Oh, no, look at my family and I am just going to turn out like them'. It is things like that where you are constantly not purposely but constantly just giving them confidence and just giving them self esteem and just and I think that is why I did ... it was just to kind of realise more their potential and to just kind of encourage things that they are good at and ...
(Befriending)

By contrast, the following quotation from a key worker highlighted how she believed that she had to take a very direct approach by challenging the behaviour of the young person before they could progress:

Well we have our ups and downs. When I started working with her she was just so loud and all over the place and I thought how am I going to [work round] this. I realised that I couldn't pussyfoot around with her and be nice to her and let her off with things because it wouldn't work. She needs a relationship where I am strong, not telling her off but putting her in her place when she needs to be put in her place because she used to be all over the shop – she used to scream and shout and ye ken, be really loud and just like a child of six. And it's taken a long time to make her see that that wasn't normal, that this is not how you behave when you are out and about and in public.

Another befriender felt that the intervention allowed the young person to 'try on' an alternative identity, which would be risky in front of his peers:

That is when he is indoors but when you get really on to his good side and you take him out of the home environment and away from his friends' environment as I say it is a different [boy]. I think he finds he has to have this brave macho front kind of in front of his friends and things like that.
(Befriending)

Boundaries

As in the interviews with young people, mentors claimed that the negotiation of boundaries highlighted the 'special nature of mentoring relationships'. The notion of boundaries encompassed a range of issues: from making sense of the relationship in relation to other social networks; to dealing with anxieties about how 'close' relationships between adults and young people might be misinterpreted by others; to comparison of relationships with others outwith care settings. All the projects in this study provided clear guidelines about disclosure of information by young people to members of staff. These appeared to be well understood and generally agreed, but were frequently a source of discussion and negotiation. The fragility of mentoring relationships was vividly illustrated in discussions about confidentiality within the education and housing projects. Staff in these projects often worked with other professionals and agencies on behalf of the young person and some of these were less flexible. For example, a worker from another agency who was interviewed for this study, voiced a perception that project workers in the housing project were effective in reaching out to difficult groups of young people but that some were unclear about limits and about helping young people to develop a realistic understanding of the skills required to sustain a tenancy.

Mentors regarded pragmatism and creativity as necessary: for key workers, flexibility and discretion was constantly called for, leading one key worker to declare that blanket agreements were unhelpful in many situations:

There are things like child protection and stuff that you have got to pass on. I suppose if she told me like shop lifting ... then maybe I wouldn't be rushing to the police and saying this is what they're doing but that's the kind of thing you work on 'what's going to happen if you get caught doing that?' Legally you probably should pass it on but you [would say goodbye to having any kind of] a relationship if you did ... it is very much on a ... you treat each one as it comes and deal with it as it unfolds.
(Education)

A key worker in the housing project pointed out that reporting all disclosures of under-age sexual activity to the police would involve project staff in permanent attendance at the police station as well as undermining relationships with young people. Judgements on a wide range of issues were made on the best available evidence and in the light of issues of consent and age. In some cases information would be shared with social workers or other professionals. Occasionally information usually shared with parents was held back in order to protect the young person and at other times, parents were seen as worthy of protection. In some instances, the preservation of confidentiality was a means of reinforcing the 'special' nature of the relationship. In the following example, the mentor explained that she often had a cup of tea with Scott's mother and was invited to the house, even though she no longer was his official key worker:

... like I would never tell her what is happening in here but Scott always says, don't tell that to my mum and like I won't say anything, you know so it is like and she will go on about his behaviour there and he'll be, 'oh shut up mum' and I'm [laughing] 'oh aye, just wait till we get back' teasing him.
(Education)

Befrienders were less likely to refer to disclosure as an issue that arose in their relationships. This is perhaps related to the ways in which befriending relationships were constructed as more 'occasional' and less connected to other social networks. Many befrienders felt that dealing with sensitive issues went beyond their remit and their capability. Difficulties in these areas would be brought to the co-ordinator who would then negotiate with families and other professionals where necessary.

Professional friends?

The accounts given by befrienders suggested that their role was as a 'friend' who listens and challenges but has set limits in terms of 'professional' skills. Some befrienders likened their role to a relationship with an aunt or granny. By contrast, paid workers focused on developing a trusting relationship, which could then act as a mechanism for promoting changes in behaviour and were less likely to describe the relationship as one akin to friendship.

Whereas young people were likely to describe mentoring relationships as going beyond professional boundaries, mentors largely viewed their mentoring as a working relationship. Thus when young people occasionally visited workers at home, mentors claimed that this was carefully organised and structured to demonstrate that this was a 'special' occasion. A few key workers agreed that they took a flexible approach to this, making themselves available in evenings and outside the project. For one key worker, it was in exceptional circumstances that this happened, as for instance when one young person was pregnant or going through a 'rough patch'. One worker found that despite her attempts, young people succeeded in finding her home number, but she claimed that this was rarely abused. A number of key workers felt that clear demarcation was necessary to protect their privacy and to ensure that they could 'switch off'. Nevertheless lifts would be offered, people would bump into each other on the street or meet in the local shopping centre. In this respect, the mentoring assumed a neighbourly or community feel, offering a known face to talk to in the street. This was more difficult in a city setting, where befrienders and young people moved in different circles and areas of the city.

Underlying processes

Dilemmas in one-to-one befriending

Within one-to-one mentoring at the befriending project, the private nature of the relationship brought some dilemmas. It provided flexibility for relationships to develop and a sense of ownership for young people over their personalised relationship with their volunteer. The co-ordinator played a key role in monitoring relationships and acted as a link for both young person and befriender. However, a major tension was that the private nature of the relationship itself meant that the co-ordinator did not always have early access to information about emerging difficulties. The staff were well aware of the need for measures to safeguard young people against harm within such private relationships.

For some mentors, the limitations of one-to-one mentoring were also identified. Within the befriending project, many befrienders had gone through a process of rationalisation from what had been fairly grandiose hopes to what they viewed as much more realistic possibilities:

> ... it just didna' work out and I was quite
> disappointed, but then I think I went in with high
> hopes and maybe too much expectation on my part
> maybe. Maybe that is what it was but as I say I have
> learnt since then.
> (Befriending)

Time

All mentors acknowledged that relationships were likely to be time limited. Key workers frequently claimed that they did not get involved emotionally,

but this seemed to pose a great deal of difficulty in some cases. Key workers frequently referred to the need to balance their commitment to an individual young person without creating long-term dependency. For some key workers this meant giving the relationship enough time to work through issues and sometimes to repair damage from the past. For others the nature of the issues facing the young person might be viewed as demanding more frequent sessions or longer meeting periods. The timespan of interventions was also a concern for mentors and this was often linked to discussion of perceptions about 'appropriate' relationships and in particular the implications of emotional involvement as discussed above. The use of a team approach was seen as helping to deal with this issue. Key workers were more likely to point to other demands such as paperwork, meetings with other professionals and attendance at reviews as taking time away from developing the relationship itself.

The opportunity to develop relationships with an open-ended timescale was viewed as vital to this befriender:

> I think from the youngster's point of view, it might be
> nice to think that whatever's supportive and so on is
> not just going to be chopped off. I mean the
> youngsters are all aware of the hearing system and
> how it finishes at 16 and all the rest of it and that's
> your provision, goodbye.
> (Befriending)

Others viewed the challenges that faced the young people as deep-seated and as demanding approaches that would allow the young person to go at their own pace:

> ... it is not instant with her. You couldna wave a magic
> wand and say well this is what we want to do with
> her and we will do it and it will be done within a
> week. You couldn't. Because she doesn't work that
> way and she needs time to kind of adjust and it takes
> a long time for some things to sink in and for her to

realise what she is doing. And she needs reminding all the time and you have to be on her back all the time about swearing and stuff like that. And if you are constantly going on about it over a lengthy time, like six months or a year, it has sunk in and she knows when it is ok to swear and when not to swear and you couldn't do it instantly. She is just not that kind of person and I think with the majority of the young people in here, they need time to adjust, and move on.
(Education)

For one befriender, timing became an issue that led him to take unilateral action. He believed that a weekly meeting was insufficient to enable him to offer an adequate level of support; this led him to make his own decisions, which he neglected to discuss with the co-ordinator. Thus his additional time with the young person was a private arrangement which was not subject to the monitoring and assessment of the project. The co-ordinator pointed out that additional meetings were not prohibited by the project but that they had to be negotiated. Clearly an informal mentoring relationship allows for such development but within a planned mentoring programme this may be at odds with existing guidelines and protocols. Such an incident highlighted the difficult balance required of the co-ordinator in keeping tabs on volunteer activity while allowing the relationship to develop between the befriender and the young person.

Overall, befrienders and key workers were well aware that in working with vulnerable young people, 'quick fixes' offered little solution to the challenges that were faced. For some, the work that they were engaged in aimed to mitigate the ill effects of poor professional and parental decisions and stop-gap approaches to working with young people.

Endings
For many mentors the ending of a relationship presented similar difficulties to those identified by young people in the previous chapter. For those relationships that failed to develop, endings could represent frustration and a sense of failure:

You like to think that you make a difference for everybody but there's some of them you just can't get to and you've just got to accept that. It is frustrating and it is soul destroying.
(Housing)

At other times, a relationship might be ended by staff if it was viewed as either too intense or as failing to thrive:

… the senior staff can see if somebody is getting too close that it's time to split. That could be a case of changing key worker as well as the personality not getting on, getting on too well because you definitely need, I feel a line where the young person has got to feel comfortable with the key worker but I don't think it should be too close. There should still be the distinction that they are the member of staff.
(Education)

But this was not always a clear cut process. Within the housing project, one worker retained contact with one young woman who was banned from the house due to her behaviour. Although she had moved to another post outwith the project but still in the agency, this key worker continued to work with the young woman, as she felt that she could help mediate with other professionals to ensure she got access to services.

For many befrienders, the ending of a relationship represented a sense of personal loss, especially when, as in this example, the young person had taken the decision to move out of the relationship:

Well, on the one hand rather sad and disappointed but, on the other hand, if he is feeling that he has moved on, then [pauses] that is fine. I am just not sure how things are for him.
(Befriending)

Within the education project, leaving school usually represented a cut-off point, although commitment to some participants was continued. For some who left, a celebration was used to mark the moving on, with cakes and a party. More often, young people drifted off, attending more irregularly, sometimes into work or just living more at home. Within the housing project, the move to independent living did not necessarily imply the ending of a mentoring relationship, but it certainly moved into another gear. Where young people were evicted or sent to prison, the key workers retained no contact or only kept in touch through young people's own networks.

Gender issues

Many mentors pointed towards the need, as they saw it, for a young person to have a trusting relationship with an adult female or another male. This was often described as necessary due to the perceived inadequacy within the family or neighbourhood networks. Accounts given by both key workers and befrienders indicated strongly-held assumptions about appropriate sex roles and family responsibilities. A number of women key workers pointed out that young people specifically referred to them as 'mum' for example. Some viewed this in a positive light as demonstrating both the significance of the relationship for the young person and that the relationship went beyond conventional professional boundaries.

Intuitively, many mentors felt positively about a young person having a relationship with an older adult; however, this was often tempered by questions concerning how the legitimacy of the relationship would be viewed, particularly for men. Male befrienders and key workers expressed a fear that they might be perceived as over-involved with young men in particular and described a number of strategies to ensure they were rarely alone with their charges. For many mentors of both sexes, articulating their feelings about relationships was extremely difficult, which perhaps highlights some of these tensions.

Styles of mentoring

The predominant style of mentoring in this study was that of an *individual* relationship between an adult and a young person. The befriending project generally offered this form of support, although some young people attended group events. The paid workers in the befriending project also played a key role in providing a safety net for young people and befrienders in what was inevitably a highly privatised relationship. A major tension was that the private nature of the relationship itself meant that the co-ordinator did not always have early access to information about emerging difficulties. The staff were well aware of the need for measures to safeguard young people against harm within such private relationships.

However it was clear that other styles were also in use. For example, *team mentoring* was evident within the education and the housing projects. Here a staff group or team of workers provided mentoring support and this took place individually or with groups of young people and in some instances, a mixture of the two. For some young people this meant there was an array of potential support and mentoring available to them. Others preferred to work with one individual, often in an attempt to ensure control over the flow of information about their lives.

Within all the projects, young people, particularly young women, pointed to the role of *peer mentoring*. People close to their own age who had themselves 'been through the mill' often provided advice and examples of being successful in moving out of a criminal career, developing a stable family, holding down a job or dealing with mental health problems. Scope for peer mentoring within the befriending project was much more limited (although this took place within the associated group work projects).

Peer mentoring usually took place within the wider social networks of young people. Typically young women's mentors were young mothers who had their own house or flat and who were bringing up a child. Often they were described as having settled down. Another version of this was the successful graduates of the projects who had managed to continue their college course or hold down a job but who were still seen as part of the group.

Among young women, *best friend mentoring* was also referred to as an important source of support and critical friendship. For two who had lived in the housing project, their moves to independent living led to less face-to-face contact so that the relationship was largely based on texting and telephone conversations.

In many cases then, planned mentoring relationships existed alongside informal mentoring relationships with other workers or within their peer group, best friend or with a team of workers.

Key points

- Mentors from all projects valued the chance to work with rather than on young people.

- Many drew on their own experiences and backgrounds to guide their work.

- Mentors frequently viewed their role as re-socialising young people and for some this was based on trying to 'normalise' behaviour.

- Many pointed to the resilience, strengths and capacity of vulnerable young people.

- Befrienders emphasised the social nature of their role, while key workers were more concerned with changing behaviour.

- Suspicion and ambivalence were expressed regarding the role of peer groups in undermining their work.

- All viewed their role as a bridge to more formal professional roles.

- The processes of building a mentoring relationship were described as demanding consistency, flexibility and a mix of support and challenge.

- Setting boundaries was a delicate process for key workers and one where sensitivity to individual cases had to be considered.

- Dilemmas in managing one-to-one relationships were evident.

- Mentors were more likely to view their role as falling within a professional framework rather than as 'special relationships'.

7 Conclusions and implications

This concluding chapter focuses on key issues that have arisen from this study and the implications of these for programmes of planned mentoring.

The versions of planned mentoring interventions explored in this study were highly valued by many young people and those working with them, whether they were paid key workers or unpaid volunteers. However the extent to which the intervention contributed to the ability of groups of vulnerable young people to reflect on and address the issues facing them is a much more complex issue.

It is clear that planned mentoring is not a 'magic bullet' that is capable of solving all the problems facing young people and those charged with working with them. Structural constraints continue to exert a powerful influence on the trajectories of such vulnerable young people: the influence of poverty, early childhood difficulties and inequalities in health impacted strongly on the lives of young people in this sample. Such issues cannot be offset solely by good relationships with adults or anyone else. The development of a mentoring relationship, however, may enhance the capacity to reflect on these issues and to be better able to negotiate services and support in certain circumstances. For example, within the befriending project this was likely to be through improved ability to negotiate difficult family circumstances, while within the other projects success was more likely to be in terms of reintegration into the mainstream.

Such capacity is a characteristic of resilience, a concept that is often drawn on to explain how some young people construct buffers against the ill effects of bad experiences. We are still in the early stages of understanding resilience and how it may promote 'steeling mechanisms' for young people. This study suggests a need to extend the study of resilience to examine how young people develop strategies both individually and collectively and the role of mentoring within these. This question needs examination longitudinally, as much with those who do not succeed in conventional terms as with those who do. This study provides some evidence that the capacity to accept mentoring support is a valuable mechanism in building up resilience and expertise within different sets of relationships. Gains from mentoring may be apparent in the long term as opposed to the short term and may even be cross generational. Although it was not a mentoring programme per se, findings from the High Scope/Perry preschool enrichment study in the USA are relevant here. Twenty years after the study was undertaken, considerable long-term benefits have been evident from this pre-school programme in the variety of pro-social behaviours and in the ways that participants in the study interacted with their own children. Within the study reported here, a number of young people expressed the intention to use their experiences of mentoring in future employment, in bringing up their own children and in developing their own careers.

This also relates to the ways in which key workers and befrienders perceived their roles. Key workers described themselves as developing an approach to 'normalise' the behaviour of some young people. This was done through role modelling, through demonstrating different lifestyles and ways of coping and by establishing clear boundaries and codes of behaviour that workers felt had not been part of some young people's family socialisation. In this respect mentoring was framed as a process decided by the adults, and it was the pace of the intervention that was negotiated with the young person. However in practice this was a less linear process, with a sharing of skills, negotiation of roles and subversion of boundaries by young people through the processes of negotiation.

The respective merits of paid and unpaid mentoring require some teasing out. In key respects, the sample of young people from the befriending project differed from those working with the housing and education projects in that they were younger and likely to be referred due to family disruption. It may be most useful to look at mentoring as a spectrum of intensity, with volunteer befrienders offering a form of mentoring that focuses on respite and opportunities for shared activity with less troubled or younger children. The voluntary commitment of the befrienders was an important element in making the relationship 'special' and developing the potential for friendship. Equally it is true that relationships could become isolated if befrienders were unwilling to participate in further events, despite the best efforts of the co-ordinator. Better resourcing to develop and integrate individual befriending pairs into community or neighbourhood initiatives could help mitigate the isolation of individual pairs. It might also enable a narrowing of the social distance between befrienders and young people.

At the other end of the spectrum both housing and education projects offered a higher dosage of mentoring that ultimately aimed to reintegrate the young people into the main-stream. Many of the young people had a complex array of difficulties and had contact with a range of professionals with whom mentors often acted as advocates. Unexpectedly the status of paid workers did not appear to distance them from their clients although it made for more problematic relationships with other professionals. This is very different from the 'engagement' mentoring that Colley describes in that it is a relationship grounded in the negotiation between young people and mentors, highly demanding of time, skill and tact. It also implied a knowledge and understanding of the local context, patterns of exclusion and community. Such an intensive level of support is unlikely to be possible within a voluntary context. Paradoxically it also demands some of the flexibility of voluntary commitment in promoting a version of 'professional *friendship*'.

The long-term agenda of encouraging young people to undertake self-surveillance and modify their behaviour raises important questions about young people's self-agency and capacity to negotiate. Within the education project, it was clear that the quest for normalisation meant that young people were encouraged to set realistic goals and to make their horizons manageable. While this was important in helping young people to achieve, it was double-edged in encouraging conformity to dominant sets of values and aspirations. The imperative to 'fit in' to normal life left little opportunity to reflect critically on the lack of opportunities, the structural constraints or indeed to think beyond their immediate area and localised interests. Striking a balance between raising false hopes and lowering expectations is a continuing issue for those working with vulnerable young people. However, mentoring processes may offer an opportunity to tackle this through building relationships which can act both as a launch pad and as a safety net. However this demands a long-term commitment on the part of mentors in order to support young people to feel safe enough to take risks, to fail and to start again. It also requires the other agencies and institutions with which such young people interact to adopt more flexible approaches and to adopt a 'mentor rich' approach.

There is some contradiction in an intervention that aims to promote better social relationships through an individual relationship with one adult. This is particularly problematic when we consider the highly social behaviour of most young people. Within the education project, the mix of group and individual work opened up the potential for working with peer groups. Whether or not these peer groups are viewed as bad influences on individuals, the reality was that moving out from the peer group posed challenges to many vulnerable young people, particularly in small localities. Supporting young people to negotiate within peer groups and friendship groups may therefore offer greater potential in the long term than a narrow focus on individuals.

It is also clear that entering into a mentoring relationship involved some trade-offs on the part of both partners. Within the housing project, young people traded off their privacy and their autonomy in order to develop a meaningful mentoring relationship with a key worker. In exchange the worker provided social support, a form of friendship and time to explore sensitive issues in a safe context. Para-professionals, such as those working in the education project, traded off professional distance in favour of a personalised approach, which enabled good rapport to be established with many young people. However this provoked dilemmas for key workers in managing what amounted to 'professional friendships'. Much of this work took them into uncharted territory where limits were constantly under pressure. By contrast, befrienders appeared to be more reluctant to move out of the planned approach.

For befrienders, risks included the fear of being drawn into the range of problems facing families as well as young people and many were anxious to resist pressure to extend their roles. Some relationships were short lived and came to messy endings due to mismatches in expectations. In such cases, young people and befrienders expressed disillusionment about the value of the intervention. This suggests that the introduction of an adult into the social network may have unforseen outcomes in terms of 'emotional labour' that are difficult to anticipate in training programmes.

Work with families was viewed with some ambivalence by those involved in all the projects, but where this did occur, it appeared to enhance relationships. Moreover, drawing young people away from their families would seem counter-productive given the evidence in this study that, however destructive family relationships might be, young people persevered against considerable odds in retaining and improving contact. Parents interviewed in this study identified clear needs for support but found it difficult to access this outside of a specific crisis, particularly when children reached the age of 16. They reported positive contact with the projects although this was usually informal and ad hoc. Both key workers and befrienders were faced with difficulties here: many young people actively wanted to establish relationships that were independent of their families, partly in order to reflect on what was going on there within a safe climate. The establishment of mentoring for parents might prove a useful means of offering support and assistance in their attempts to negotiate both with young people and professionals, as suggested by Rhodes from her work in the USA (2002).

The implications of these findings suggest a need to explore dimensions of mentoring as an element of training for a wide array of professionals, para-professionals and volunteers. While it may be of value in specific mentoring projects, more value could be accrued from building it into practice more generally. Informal mentoring can occur within a range of relationships and settings in everyday life. It is evident that young people in this study valued being able to select mentoring support within the 'mentor rich' aspect of the housing and education interventions. Thus the relationship with the key worker was supplemented by others with workers and sometimes relatives and friends. This option was less open within the befriending project, which by its nature focused more clearly on individuals, although some befrienders made considerable efforts to support the development of relationships with others. However this suggests there is a need to develop training on mentoring for a wide range of professional fields. This needs to extend beyond acknowledging that significant relationships can be built up between professionals and young people. Better understanding of the implications of such relationships, the social contexts, the need for boundaries, the negotiation processes and the time commitment requires to be incorporated into such training.

None of the projects investigated was a mentoring project per se, although mentoring formed a major element of their remit. Nevertheless the planned mentoring within the projects has yielded important insights into the concept and suggests that mentoring provides a fruitful approach to work with vulnerable young people. However, development of the concept demands careful planning and a flexibility of approach over a considerable period of time. It is clear from the findings of this study that a 'one size fits all' template with a pre-determined agenda would have very limited application in relation to the young people sampled in this study. Thus well planned and supported befriending relationships can offer straightforward support and respite, which appeals to many young people in difficulties and to volunteers with experience and time. The version of mentoring offered in the housing and education projects, appears to offer some potential for very vulnerable young people to develop a stable and manageable independence, through the negotiation of meaningful relationships over time.

References

Clayden, J. and Stein, M. (2002) *Mentoring for Careleavers. Evaluation Report.* (May). University of York: Prince's Trust

Coles, B. (2001) *Joined Up Youth Research, Policy and Practice.* Leicester: Youth Work Press/Barnardo's

Colley, H. (2001) 'Righting rewritings of the myth of mentor: a critical perspective on career guidance mentoring', *British Journal of Guidance and Counselling,* Vol. 29, No. 2, pp. 177–97

Colley, H. (2003) 'Engagement mentoring for socially excluded youth: problematising and 'holistic' approach to creating employability through the transformation of habitus', *British Journal of Guidance and Counselling,* Vol. 31, No. 1, pp. 77–101.

Colley, H. (2003) *Mentoring for Social Inclusion.* London: Routledge

Forrest, D. (1999) *Moray Youth Action's 16–18 Employment Initiative: a social justice evaluation.* Elgin: Aberlour Childcare Trust

Forrest, K. (2002) *Befriending Young People: the fostering or loaning of friendship: a qualitative study exploring befrienders' experience.* Unpublished MLitt Thesis. Aberdeen: University of Aberdeen

Furlong, A. and Cartmel, F. (1997) *Young People and Social Change; individualisation and risk in late modernity.* Milton Keynes: Open University Press

Herrera, C., Sipe, C.L. and Mclanahan, W.S. (2000) *Mentoring School Age Children: relationship development in community based and school based programs.* Philadelphia: Public/Private Ventures

Mason, P., Webster, C., Johnson, L., Macdonald, R. and Ridley, L. (2000) *Snakes and Ladders: young people, transitions and social exclusion.* Paper presented at the Youth 2000 Conference, Keele University (September)

Millburn, T., Rowlands, C., Stephen, S., Woodhouse, H. and Sneider, A. (2003) *Step it Up … Charting Young People's Progress; the report of the national development project entitled Defining the Purpose of Youth Work and Measuring Performance.* Glasgow: University of Strathclyde/Prince's Trust, Scottish Executive

National Youth Agency (NYA) (1999) *Collected Papers from National Research and Policy Seminar on Youth Mentoring.* Leicester: National Youth Agency/Joseph Rowntree Foundation/DfEE

Philip, K. (1997) *New Perspectives on Mentoring; young people, youth work and adults.* Unpublished PhD Thesis. Aberdeen: University of Aberdeen

Philip, K. (2000) *A Literature Review on Youth Mentoring for the Joseph Rowntree Foundation.* Aberdeen: Centre for Educational Research, University of Aberdeen

Philip, K. (2003) 'Youth mentoring: the American dream comes to the UK?', *British Journal of Guidance and Counselling,* Vol. 31, No. 1, pp. 101–12

Philip, K. and Hendry, L.B. (1996) 'Young people and mentoring: towards a typology?', *Journal of Adolescence,* Vol. 19, pp. 189–201.

Philip, K. and Hendry, L.B. (2000) 'Making sense of mentoring or mentoring making sense? Reflections on the mentoring process by adult mentors with young people', *Journal of Community and Applied Social Psychology,* Vol. 10, pp. 211–23.

Rhodes, J. (2002) *Stand By Me: the risks and rewards of mentoring today's youth.* New York: Harvard University Press

Scottish Executive (2003) *A Partnership for a Better Scotland: partnership agreement.* Retrieved from http://www.scotland.gov.uk/library5/governemnt.pfbs-04.asp

Shucksmith, J. and Hendry, L.B. (1998) *Health Issues and Adolescents: Growing Up and Speaking Out.* London: Routledge

Skinner, A. and Fleming, J. (1999) *Mentoring Socially Excluded Young People: lessons from practice.* Manchester: National Mentoring Network

Sharing a laugh?